improve your
endgame play

GLENN FLEAR

EVERYMAN CHESS

Gloucester Publishers plc   www.everymanchess.com

First published in 2000 by Gloucester Publishers plc (formerly Everyman
Publishers plc), Northburgh House, 10 Northburgh Street, London EC1V
0AT.

British Library Cataloguing-in-Publication Data
A catalogue record for this book is available from the British Library.

ISBN 978 1 85744 246 5

Distributed in North America by The Globe Pequot Press, P.O Box 480,
246 Goose Lane, Guilford, CT 06437-0480.

All other sales enquiries should be directed to Everyman Chess, Northburgh
House, 10 Northburgh Street, London EC1V 0AT
tel: 020 7253 7887 fax: 020 7490 3708
email: info@everymanchess.com; website: www.everymanchess.com

To the *Flear boys*: Derek, my father and my sons James and Nathan.

EVERYMAN CHESS SERIES (formerly Cadogan Chess)
Chief advisor: Byron Jacobs
Commissioning editor: John Emms
Assistant editor: Richard Palliser

Typeset and edited by First Rank Publishing, Brighton
Cover design by Horacio Monteverde
Printed and bound in the US.

Contents

Chapter One

Important Endgame Themes

- How do We improve Our Endgame Play?
- Entering the Endgame
- The Role of the King
- Zugzwang
- Drawing Techniques
- Winning Techniques
- Try it Yourself

How do We improve Our Endgame Play?

All experienced players have gradually developed their endgame knowledge over time. This has come about through them playing, analysing and studying all aspects of the game including endgames. It's significant that, when asked how to improve one's chess, the top players generally reply 'study endgames!' How should we do this? This book tries to give method to the madness of this process!

There are specialised books containing dozens, if not hundreds, of theoretical endgame positions. If we try and learn these, one-by-one, with all the exceptions to general rules and related positions, we soon become bored, exhausted and confused. What's worse, we tend to forget. A dispiriting exercise!

The Grandmasters of today did not become proficient at endgames by spending all their time learning by heart seemingly improbable and obscure endgame theory from dusty old tomes.

No! There must be a more pleasant and realistic way especially as time is limited for the majority of amateurs, who naturally want to improve and are willing to make some effort, but have other things to do in life as well!

Most young players only study openings, but why? They study an opening because they hope to have a chance to play it; either the exact moves that they have learned or the same ideas and principles in an analogous variation. Why do we chose a certain opening? Probably because it looks interesting, a friend plays it or we saw it played and analysed from the last World Championship match.

So, why not do the same with endings? If you or a friend have an interesting ending, or see one in a Kasparov game, for example, spend some time analysing the critical moments. Later, at home, look up in books similar positions or simplified positions that could have occurred in the analysis. In my youth, a friend and I used to set each other a few endgame tests – this was fun and didn't do either of us any harm, he became an International Master in later years!

In endings, some positions crop up time and time again, whereas others are not exactly the same as the ones we know but require the application of ideas and manoeuvres that we have come across in our own experience. I think the most important way to improve in chess is to continue to *enjoy it*! To enjoy endgames most of us need to see the practical importance of our efforts.

There are a certain number of techniques and basic positions that need to be learnt and I have covered many of them here. I have also chosen a number of examples to illustrate principles and to show how some basic knowledge is then applied in practice. There are some exercises to test and stimulate memory and the thinking processes that enable us to solve practical problems. However, most of all I hope that you enjoy reading and studying the book and this will ultimately improve your endgame play.

Entering the Endgame

The endgame generally refers to positions with less pieces, but...

WARNING: Less pieces or a simplified position doesn't necessarily mean a simple position! Don't be lured into the trap of playing too quickly or superficially.

Below, there are a few examples to get our teeth into, but first of all there are some general points to keep in mind as the story unfolds.

In the middlegame, tension and interaction between the forces can be very tense. After a number of exchanges leading to the ending other considerations come to the fore. It's important to take stock and adjust yourself to the new, perhaps radically different position.

TIP: Even if your next move or plan seems ever so obvious, make a point of investing a little time to cool down and view the present board position afresh. Or, put more simply 'sit on your hands!'

There are still 64 squares but less pieces on each side to cover them, so each piece needs to be found a role including and, especially, the king. This represents a change of strategy from the opening and middlegame where one of the foremost aims is to keep the monarch as far away as possible from the battlefield.

TIP: Bear in mind the idea of improving your worst-placed or least effective piece, how does this compare with the obvious move that your hand wants to play instantly?

Checkmate by direct means is rarely the sensible plan with few pieces on the board, so what is the appropriate plan? Common plans include creating and pushing passed pawns towards the queening square; invading your opponent's territory to cause havoc amongst his pawns; restricting the mobility of your opponent's pieces and pawns; fighting for control of crucial squares or simply exchanging further pieces.

Time for some examples. Let's start by thinking about your most important piece.

The Role of the King in Defence and Attack

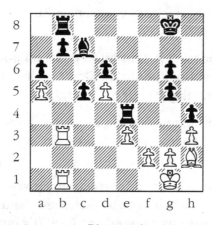

Diagram 1

The king in a defensive role

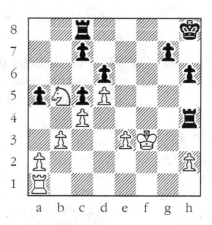

Diagram 2

The king in an attacking role

In Diagram 1, Flear-Miezis, Gonfreville 1999, I continued **30 Kf1** Not 30 Rxb7?? Rxb7 31 Rxb7 Rb4 and Black wins! The monarch is brought towards the centre where it is to play an important role in holding up Black's passed pawn or pawns. **30...c4 31 Rxb7 Rc8 32 Ke2 Bxa5 33 Bxd6 c3 34 Rb8** Playing for mate with 34 Rd7? c2 35 Rbb7 fails to 35...Bc3. The exchange of a pair of rooks enhances the power of the centralised king. **34...Ree8 35 Rxc8 Rxc8 36 Be5 Rc5 37 e4 Rb5** Otherwise White continues with Kd3, Rc1 and picks off the isolated c-pawn. **38 Rxb5 axb5 39 Kd3 b4 40 Kc2** The king totally stymies the black pawns whereas White can take his time to force through a pawn to promote. **40...Kf7 41 Bd6 Ke8 42 Bc5 Kd7 43 e5 Kc7 44 e6 Kc8 45 Be7 Kb7 46 d6 Kc6 47 d7 1-0**

In the example Capablanca-Corzo, Havana 1901 (Diagram 2), Capablanca clouds the issue in a seemingly hopeless ending, by activating his king. **34 Kg3** Black could also improve his own king by playing 34...g5 followed by 35...Kg7. It is noticeable that Corzo 'never gets around' to bringing his own king into play. **34...Re4 35 Re1 Re7 36 e4 Rf8 37 Na7 g5 38 Nc6 Ree8 39 e5** An interesting try. The exchanges expose Black's queen-side pawns, harrying him and not giving him time to... central-ise his king. **39...dxe5 40 Rxe5 Rxe5 41 Nxe5 Re8 42 Nd7 Re2 43 a4 Re3+ 44 Kg4 Rxb3 45 Kf5 Rb4 46 Ne5 Rxa4 47 Ke6 Rb4 48 Kd7 Rb7 49 Nd3 a4 50 Kc8** White's king is mak-ing a nuisance of itself! **50...Rb1 51 Kxc7 Rd1 52 Nxc5 a3 53 d6 a2?** 53...g4 for the record, would still win. **54 Nb3 g4 55 d7 h5 56 d8Q+ Rxd8 57 Kxd8 h4 58 c5 g3 59 hxg3 hxg3 60 c6 g2 61 c7** ½-½

TIP: Don't forget to use your king in the ending. The monarch is an excellent piece for invading the enemy camp, winning pawns and supporting a passed pawn.

Zugzwang

Diagram 3
The game is won using 'zugzwang'!

In chess it is not possible to say to your opponent 'I'd rather not move, go ahead and please have another turn!' you have to have your turn if it pleases you or not.

In this position, Black to play must release the defence of the c-pawn and so loses the pawn and, in a few moves, the game. White to play has the winning move **1 Kd7** ... not really changing the character of the position but putting his opponent in a deadly zugzwang. **1...Kb8 2 Kxc6 Kc8 3 Kb6 Kb8 4 c6 Kc8** 4...Ka8 sets a stalemate trap but 5 Kc7! Ka7 6 Kd7 Kb6 7 c7 queens without further incident. **5 c7 Kd7 6 Kb7 Kd6 7 c8Q etc.**

TIP: Look out for potential zugzwangs, particularly when pieces have a restricted scope for action. For instance, when they are defending squares and pawns.

Diagram 4
Zugzwang in action

Black wins in Flear-Moskalenko, Fuerteventura 1992, with a passing move, a useful weapon in endings. **54...Kh7!** All White's pieces are defended, but after this excellent move, he *must* move something and in fact he loses material by force. **55 Rg2** Neither 55 Bg4 Qh4+ 56 Kg2 Qxg4+ nor 55 Bh5 Qh4+ 56 Kg2 Qg5+! 57 Kf2 Qxh5 are any better. **55...Qf1+ 56 Kh2** The point is that 56 Rg1 Qh3 is mate. **56...Qxd1** The position is a win for Black, but White can still try to make a fight of it.

TIP: If your opponent's pieces are on their best defensive squares and you can't find a way through, look for a way of 'passing' and obliging him to yield ground or material.

Simple Drawing Techniques

The following are basic techniques for holding a worse endgame.

Stalemate Traps

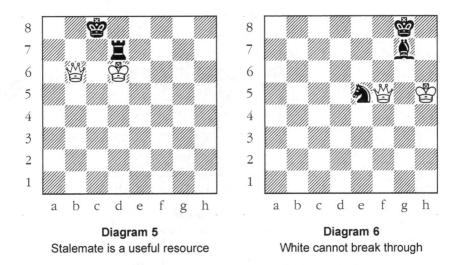

Diagram 5	Diagram 6
Stalemate is a useful resource	White cannot break through

Be aware of stalemate particularly when the opponent's king is on the edge and has virtually no squares. In Diagram 5 the white queen is a knight's move away from the black king, not necessarily a bad thing, but it should send a danger signal that stalemate traps are in the air. **1 Ke6! Re7+ 2 Kf6!** would give White an ending which can normally be won: queen versus rook. Instead 2 Kxe7? and earlier 1 Kc6 Rd6+! 2 Kxd6 are both stalemate.

WARNING: Be aware of stalemate traps when the defending king is severely restricted!

The Fortress

Diagram 6 sees an unusual position. White cannot break down the black set-up. He cannot get close enough with his king to mate or force zugzwang; we say that Black has a 'fortress'.

NOTE: Even with a material advantage it can be difficult or even impossible to win if entry (especially for the king) into the opposing camp is prevented.

Simple Winning Techniques

These techniques are useful for converting endgame advantages.

Winning by Exchanging

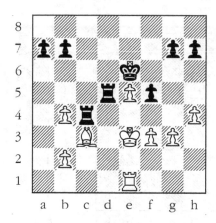

Diagram 7
Black wins by making profitable exchanges

Black has a small material advantage of the exchange for a pawn. However, White has constructed a 'fortress' and it's not obvious how Black can invade. In Lombardy-Fischer, USA Championship 1960, Fischer found a strong simplifying combination. **1...Rxc3+! 2 bxc3 Rxe5+ 3 Kd2 Rxe1 4 Kxe1** Black has only material equality but has the better placed king. **4...Kd5 5 Kd2 Kc4 6 h5 b6 7 Kc2 g5 8 h6 f4 9 g4 a5** The pawn structure is also favourable for Black who can create an 'outside passed pawn', a concept developed in Chapters Three and Four. **10 bxa5 bxa5 11 Kb2 a4 12 Ka3 Kxc3 13 Kxa4 Kd4 14 Kb4 Ke3 0-1**

 TIP: Exchanging, or even giving back, material to obtain a simplified ending is often the easiest way to win.

The Active Rook

In Janowski-Gunsberg, St Petersburg 1914 (Diagram 9), White is passive and Black hopes to create an invasion route for his king. But... **1 Rc2!** Before it's too late White abandons a pawn in order to activate his rook. Passive defence will not work, e.g. 1 fxg6 Kxg6 2 Ke2 Kf7 3 Kf2 Ke6 4 Ke2 f5 5 exf5+ Kxf5 6 Kf2

Kf4 7 Ke2 e4 8 Kf2 e3+ 9 Ke2 Ke4. **1...gxf5 2 exf5 Rxa3 3 Rc6 Kg7 4 Rc7+ Kg8 5 Rc6 Kg7 6 Rc7+** Black's king is tied to the defence of the f-pawn and he cannot make progress.

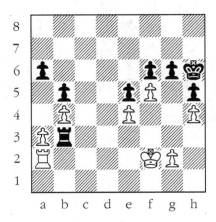

Diagram 9
White activates at the cost of a pawn

Promoting Combinations

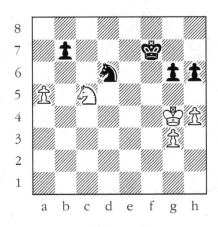

Diagram 10
White wins with a neat combination

White wins as follows: **1 Nxb7! Nxb7 2 a6 h5+ 3 Kf3!** and the pawn goes through. Sacrifices to promote pawns are common.

TIP: Advanced pawns, whether passed or not, are an important tactical factor.

Try it Yourself

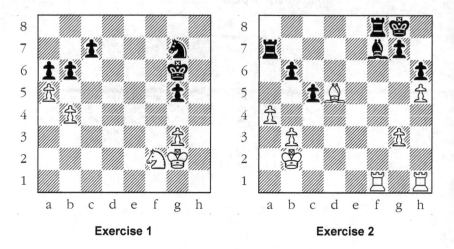

Exercise 1   **Exercise 2**

Exercise 1: White to play. What is the likely result?

Exercise 2: Material is equal and simplification is on the cards. How should White continue?

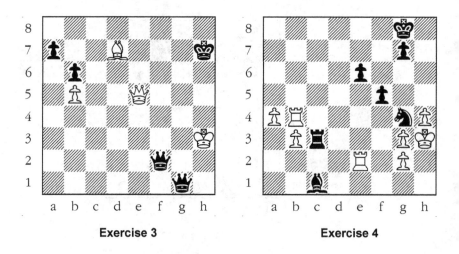

Exercise 3   **Exercise 4**

Exercise 3: White to play. What is the result?

Exercise 4: How did Black manage to win in this position?

Summary

Stay aware of tactical possibilities.

Use your king.

Make a plan for the ending.

Typical endgame plans are: promoting a pawn, zugzwang, exchanging to an easier ending.

Chapter Two

Endgames with just Pieces

■ Basic Mates – The Lone King

■ Queen versus Other Pieces

■ Rook versus Minor Piece

■ Try it Yourself

This chapter starts with a few basic mates against the lone king and ends up with some rather more difficult examples such as lone queen against lone rook. There are some important points to learn even in the more trivial positions, such as how to harmonise the forces, looking out for stalemates and being methodical, which is important especially if time is limited.

By studying the methods in the basic mates you are preparing yourself for more challenging positions.

Basic Mates – The Lone King

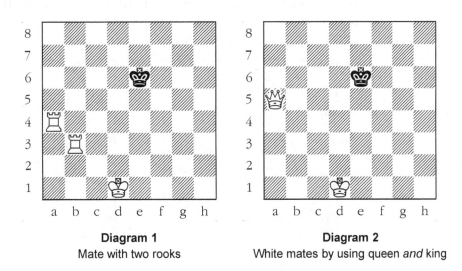

Diagram 1
Mate with two rooks

Diagram 2
White mates by using queen *and* king

To mate from Diagram 1, the king needs to be trapped against an edge of the board. One rook creates a barrier across the rank and the other, by giving check, forces the king nearer to its doom. **1 Rb5** 1 Rb6+ is a pointless check as the king advances towards the centre with 1...Kd5. **1...Kd6 2 Ra6+ Kc7 3 Rh5** Putting the rook out of reach of the black king. **3...Kb7 4 Rg6 Kc7 5 Rh7+ Kd8 6 Rg8 mate**. To give mate White didn't need to use his own king. However, in most endings with a lesser material advantage the king is required to help out.

In Diagram 2 giving lots of checks will not lead to mate. The right method is to first use the queen to limit the black king to a small sector of the board. Then the white king comes close to cover potential flight squares, freeing the queen to push the

black king towards the edge. **1 Qc5 Kd7 2 Qb6 Ke7 3 Ke2**
White could even limit further the black king with 3 Qc6.
3...Kd7 4 Ke3 Ke7 5 Ke4 Kd7 6 Ke5 Ke7 White's king covers
the squares d6, e6 and f6, thereby enabling the queen to actively push back the black monarch. **7 Qc7+ Ke8 8 Kf6 Kf8**
and White has four different mates in one.

**TIP: It's not necessary to bring the queen too close as there is
a danger of stalemate.**

Always bear in mind your opponent's next move (i.e. make sure
he has one, at least until it's checkmate!) to avoid the tragedy
(and embarrassment!) of a half-point thrown away on a silly
stalemate.

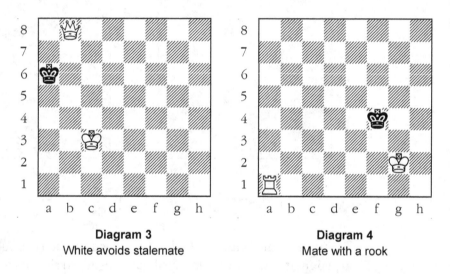

Diagram 3
White avoids stalemate

Diagram 4
Mate with a rook

In Diagram 3 if White were to blindly advance his king without
taking into account his opponent's reply he may play **1 Kb4?**
and suddenly it's stalemate! Instead 1 Kc4 is correct, anticipating 1...Ka5 2 Qb5 mate.

One of the most common endings in one's early games is rook
and king against rook (Diagram 4). The king is even more active in supporting the major piece in the gradual asphyxiation
of the opposing king. **1 Re1** Cutting the king along the e-file.
1...Kg4 Or 1...Kf5 2 Kf3 etc. **2 Re4+** White's king controls f3, g3
and h3 and the rook check forces its counterpart to cede another rank. **2...Kf5 3 Kf3** It's important to remember to defend
the rook! **3...Kg5 4 Re5+ Kg6** 4...Kh4 fails to 5 Rd5 (a passing
move) and Black is obliged to walk into mate with 5...Kh3 6

Rh5. **5 Kf4 Kf6 6 Re1** As if to say 'pass' to his opponent! Black, unable to do the same, is obliged to move to an inferior square and thus yield ground. **6...Kg6 7 Re6+ Kf7** Or 7...Kh5 when 8 Rd6 mates next move as before. **8 Kf5 Kg7 9 Re7+ Kf8 10 Kf6 Kg8 11 Kg6 Kf8 12 Re6** Again Black must move against his will. **12...Kg8 13 Re8 mate**.

The ending is not difficult if one uses the king and rook together.

NOTE: From time to time the best move is one that simply passes and forces the opponent to yield. In the ending, zugzwang, as this process is called, is an important weapon.

If you don't feel confident in winning the endings that I have examined so far, practice will help. Play this ending a few times with a friend. It will become easier as you become used to constructing a barrier, supporting with your king and using zugzwang to gain ground.

The ending of king and one minor piece (bishop or knight) is always drawn, but with two bishops the ending is won.

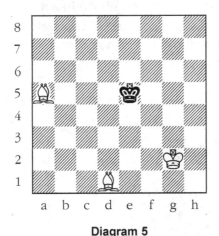

Diagram 5
All three pieces must work together

This may look tough but it uses the same ideas as above, though White has an extra piece to handle. Now White has to drive the opposing king to any corner to deliver mate. **1 Kf3 Kd4 2 Be2** Note that with one bishop on the a5-e1 diagonal and another on the a6-f1 diagonal this creates a barrier that the black king cannot pass. **2...Kd5 3 Bb6** The barrier is adjusted to further limit the prey. **3...Kc6 4 Ba7 Kd5 5 Kf4 Kd6 6 Bc4** White will obtain the e5-square for his king. **6...Kd7 7 Ke5 Ke7 8 Bd5 Kd7 9 Bc5 Kc7 10 Ke6** The black king has to go to the back rank. The next stage is to nudge him to a corner to deliver the knock-out blow (being aware of the risk of stalemate!). **10...Kd8 11 Bb6+** The black king can choose which corner but the result is the same. **11...Kc8** A similar mate results after 11...Ke8 12 Bc6+ Kf8 13 Kf6 Kg8 14 Kg6 Kh8 15 Bc5 Kg8 16 Bd5+ Kh8 17 Bd4. **12 Kd6** Bringing up the king but importantly always leaving the opposing king with a free square (here b8) until the final blow is delivered. **12...Kb8 13 Kc6 Kc8 14 Be6+ Kb8 15 Bc5** Now Black has b8 and a8 to wait, while White simply ushers over his king to oversee the execution. **15...Ka8 16 Kb6 Kb8 17 Bd6+ Ka8 18 Bd5** and mate.

TIP: Try this one out with a friend as it teaches all about co-ordinating the forces.

Queen versus Other Pieces

In the next few examples White has a queen and Black a lesser piece. What are the chances of success? In fact, with queen against minor piece the win is comfortable; the most straight-forward being against the bishop.

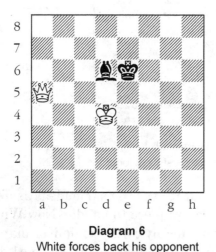

Diagram 6
White forces back his opponent

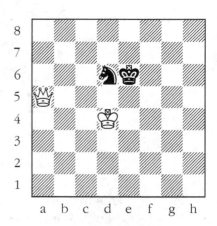

Diagram 7
Queen against knight is more tricky

In Diagram 6 after **1 Qa6 Kd7 2 Kd5** Black has no defence to the inevitable king advance on the opposite-coloured squares to those of the bishop. **2...Bc7 3 Qb7 Kd8 4 Ke6** with mate in two.

Diagram 7 presents more practical difficulties than the previous example. The knight is a useful defender on a limited front, but with careful play (watch out for forks!) White will win. **1...Nf5+ 2 Ke4 Nd6 3 Kf4 Nf7 4 Qa6+ Nd6 5 Qc6** A passing move which obliges Black to release his defensive fortress. **5...Ke7 6 Ke5 Nf7+ 7 Kd5**

TIP: Keeping the king two squares away from the knight on the diagonal will avoid annoying checks.

7...Kf8 8 Qc7 A quiet constructive move aimed at restricting the black knight's possibilities. **8...Kg8 9 Ke6 Ng5+ 10 Kf6 Nh7+ 11 Kg6 Nf8+ 12 Kh6 Ne6 13 Qe7 Nf8 14 Qg7 mate.**

It looks easy in black and white but playing it oneself can be confusing, so here are some guidelines:

1. Use the queen to restrict the opponent's pieces but place it out of the reach of forks.

2. Aim for zugzwang to oblige your opponent to give ground.

3. Use your king to limit available space for the defender and advance if possible.

The occasional knight check is not a problem if forks are avoided and the king has a target square in mind.

Queen versus Rook

Diagram 8
Losing a move

Queen versus rook is quite an advanced ending and may at first seem devilishly difficult. I have included several examples as it's an excellent ending to learn about how to constrict your opponent. The next position is one of the best examples in chess of the power of 'losing the move'.

White has made considerable progress but trying to engineer a win by brute force is difficult or impossible. Note that 1 Qa6 Rc7+ 2 Kb6 fails miserably to 2...Rc6+! and a draw due to stalemate.

The win comes quickly if White 'passes'. **1 Qe5+ Ka7 2 Qa1+ Kb8 3 Qa5** The same position, except that it is now Black to move. This proves to be more than awkward as his pieces are on their best defensive squares. In fact he now has to self-destruct. **3...Rb1** Losing immediately are 3...Re7 4 Qd8+ or 3...Rg7 4 Qe5+ and 3...Kc8 4 Qa6. More robust is 3...Rh7, but it's only a matter of a few moves before the rook drops off to a fork: 4 Qe5+ Ka8 5 Qa1+ Kb8 6 Qb1+. **4 Qe5+ Ka7 5 Qd4+ Kb8 6 Qh8+ Ka7 7 Qh7+** with a decisive fork.

Many endings require zugzwang which is why understanding such examples is important.

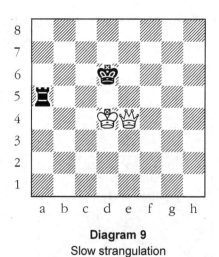

Diagram 9
Slow strangulation

Here White has to gradually push back his opponent before winning as in the previous example. The rook is a strong piece that can cut off or harass the white king, so it's necessary to limit both black pieces.

Naturally White must first avoid the threatened skewer with 1...Ra4+. **1 Qg6+** Taking the opportunity to force the black king back a rank. **1...Kd7 2 Qf6** A typical passing move. Black has to try and avoid yielding terrain. **2...Rb5** The continuation 2...Ra4+ 3 Kc5 Ra5+ 4 Kb6 helps only White. Following 2...Kc7 3 Qe6 Ra4+ 4 Kc5 Ra5+ 5 Kb4! forces a passive move from Black who dare not place his rook too far from his king due to inevitable forks, so 5...Ra7 6 Kb5 and White has again made good progress. After Black's move in the game, White again 'passes'. **3 Qf7+ Kd6 4 Qf8+ Kd7 5 Qf6 Ra5 6 Kc4** Yet again Black has to give way. **6...Kc7 7 Qe7+** Stronger than 7 Kb4 as White wishes to cover the d5-square with his queen. **7...Kc6 8 Qe6+ Kc7 9 Kb4** Squeezing! Black's hold on the fifth is broken. **9...Ra7 10 Kb5 Rb7+ 11 Kc5 Kd8** 11...Kb8 loses as in the previous example. **12 Qf6+** Bad is 12 Kc6? Rb6+! 13 Kxb6. Such stalemate traps occur when the queen is a knight's distance away from the opposing king. **12...Ke8 13 Qh8+ Kd7 14 Qg7+ Kc8 15 Qf8+ Kd7 16 Qf7+ Kc8 17 Qe8+ Kc7 18 Qa8** Black is left only with unsatisfactory rook moves. **18...Rb1** Others are no better. **19 Qc6+ Kb8 20 Qe4** Hitting the rook and leaving it with little option as forks are difficult to avoid. This has the effect of obtaining the decisive b6-square for the white king. **20...Rb7 21 Kc6 Rc7+ 22 Kb6** and mate is forced in three moves. Note that the trap 22...Rc6+ is met by 23 Kxc6.

Don't panic! This is a difficult example and should not be memorised. However, the important aspects of the play are worthy of note:

1. Using the combined efforts of king and queen to restrict and push back the black king.

2. The rook can rarely stray from its king for too long. So by gradually employing a succession of mini-zugzwangs, the rook will be obliged to release a barrier and give ground. Eventually it may be forced out into the open where it can either be forked or harassed.

3. Be aware of stalemate traps or skewers or a series of annoying checks from the rook.

4. Look for ways of improving the position of king and queen and then 'passing'. This is often more effective than direct threats or a series of pointless checks.

Rook versus Minor Piece

In the 'exchange up' endings of rook against minor piece the win is possible only in special circumstances.

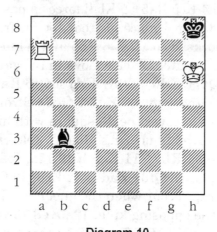

Diagram 10
Draw due to a stalemate defence

With rook against bishop the ending is normally a draw unless the defending king is badly placed. Furthermore, even when forced to the edge a draw is typical as in Diagram 10. **1 Ra8+ Bg8** gets nowhere as stalemate is threatened. If the black king were in the a8-corner then this defence would not be available.

TIP: The defending king, if forced back, should head for a 'good' corner (an opposite-coloured one to the bishop).

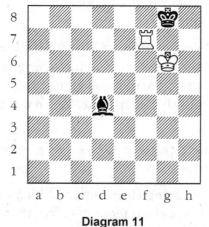

Diagram 11
Stuck in the 'bad' corner

Diagram 12
A tricky defence

In Diagram 11 Black is in the 'bad' corner and as he doesn't have the stalemate defence, his days are numbered.

White can win by creating dual threats of mate and capturing the bishop. **1 Rd7 Bb6 2 Rb7 Bc5 3 Rb8+ Bf8 4 Ra8** Black is in zugzwang and is forced to allow mate in one. **4...Kh8 5 Rxf8** mate.

In Diagram 12 Black to move finds himself in the wrong corner. **1...Kf8!** Moving away from White's mating set-up. **2 Kf6** Re-establishing the threat of mate, but now the white king is on a dark square and Black can wriggle out by giving a timely check. **2...Bb6!** 2...Ke8? moves away further from the 'bad' corner, but not for long: 3 Ke6 Kf8 4 Rf7+ Kg8 (or 4...Ke8 5 Rg7 Bc5 6 Rg8+ Bf8 7 Rh8) 5 Kf6! followed by Kg6 and Black is stuck back in the mating net of the previous example. **3 Rd6** After 3 Rb7 Bd4+ is check! The white king must move and mate will no longer be possible. **3...Ba5 4 Rd3 Ke8 5 Ke6 Kf8 6 Ra3 Bb6** and White is getting nowhere.

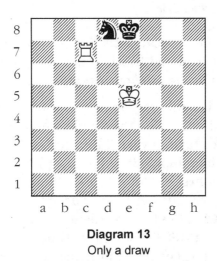

Diagram 13
Only a draw

The rook is generally not able to win against a knight if the knight doesn't stray too far from its own king or get stuck in the corner. Here White has made progress in that his opponent has been pushed back to the final rank, but still cannot win. **1 Kd6 Nf7+ 2 Ke6 Nd8+ 3 Kf6 Kf8 4 Rd7 Ke8** It pays to keep the king and knight together and to avoid leaving the king on such a dangerous square as f8 (facing the attacking white rival). For instance, 4...Nc6 fails immediately to 5 Rd6. **5 Re7+**

Kf8 6 Re1 Nb7 Precarious looking but not bad. 7 Ke6 The try
7 Rb1 should be met by 7...Nd8! (but not 7...Nd6? 8 Rb8+ Ne8+
9 Ke6 with a fatal zugzwang) 8 Rb8 Ke8 and the white king
doesn't have e6 available. 7...Ke8 8 Rb1 Nd8+ 9 Kd6 Nf7+ 10
Ke6 Nd8+ and White has not made progress.

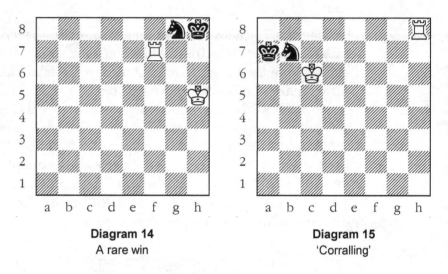

Diagram 14
A rare win

Diagram 15
'Corralling'

Here Black loses because the knight is too close to the edge of
the board. 1 Kg6 and Black doesn't have the same defence
available as in the previous example.

Here Black is badly restricted and soon succumbs. 1...Na5+ 2
Kb5 Nb7 After 2...Nb3 the knight would be fatally cut off from
its own king starting with 3 Rd8 Nc1 4 Rd2 etc. 3 Rh5! An improvement found in 1928, a modest 670 years or so after the
position was first published in an Arabian manuscript! The
move is not obvious but Black's doom is sealed, for instance:
3...Nd8 4 Rd5 Ne6 Less resilient is 4...Nb7? 5 Rd7 Kb8 6 Kb6.
5 Kc6 Kb8 6 Rd6! The knight is thus forced away from the
king. The win takes time but is inevitable. 6...Ng5 7 Rd8+ Ka7
8 Rd7+ Ka6 9 Rd3 Ka7 10 Re3 Kb8 11 Kd7 Nf7 12 Ke7 Nh6
13 Ke6 Ng4 14 Re2 Kc7 15 Kf5 Nh6+ 16 Kg6 Ng4 17 Kg5
and the stray horse is finally lassoed.

This process of mating the knight is called 'corralling'.

Try it Yourself

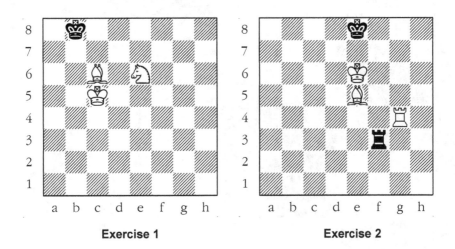

Exercise 1   Exercise 2

Exercise 1: Can you give mate? How many moves are needed?

Exercise 2: White can force a win. Can you see how?

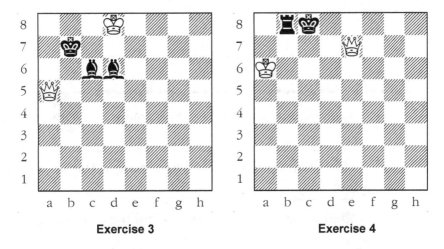

Exercise 3   Exercise 4

Exercise 3: White to move cannot make progress as 1 Qc3 is met by 1...Bc7+. Black to move loses in all variations fairly quickly. Can you find a win against the best move 1...Bb8?

Exercise 4: If it were Black to move he would lose quickly after either 1...Ra8+ 2 Kb6 Rb8+ 3 Kc6 (mating), or 1...Rb1 2 Qe6+ Kc7 3 Qf7+ Kb8 4 Qg8+ Kc7 5 Qh7+ (forking the rook). But what should White play if it is his move?

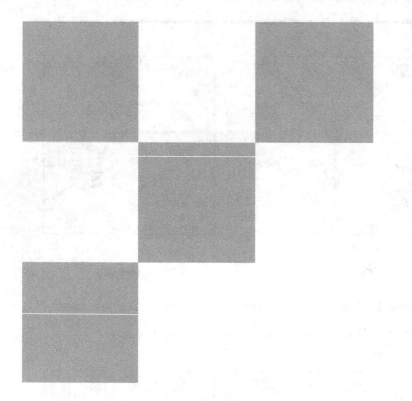

Summary

In most cases, the king is required to participate in the mating attack.

If Black has a piece it is best placed in the vicinity of its own king.

Zugzwang is often the key to making progress.

Chapter Three

Pawn Endgames

- **Converting an Extra Pawn** ■ **The Square**

- **Connected and Isolated Pawns**

- **The Opposition & King Routes**

- **The Outside Passed Pawn**

- **More Advanced Ideas**

- **Try it Yourself**

Pawn (sometimes referred to as king and pawn) endings are full of neat little ploys that render them fascinating. A thorough knowledge of basic pawn endings is essential as it is important to know whether simplification from other endings is a wise idea or not. There are a couple of general rules concerning endings that are useful to bear in mind.

TIP: With an extra pawn(s) the stronger side should seek to exchange pieces.

As pieces are exchanged the power of the extra pawn is enhanced.

Converting an Extra Pawn

An experienced player would know that a position such as the following is easily won.

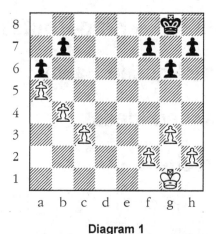

Diagram 1
The extra pawn guarantees the win

White's winning plan is as follows: he advances his king to the centre and gradually creates a passed pawn on the queenside. The white king will either support the pawn on its way to queen or, using the pawn as a diversion, will invade the kingside and consume the black pawns.

Without pieces such positions are hopeless and even resignable for experienced players. However, in the diagram position, if we gave each side a rook (or similarly a queen, or even a dark-squared bishop) the ending may not even be winning. With knights or light-squared bishops White would be favourite but there would be chances to fight.

For the unconvinced, a typical variation to show that the pawn ending is indeed grim for Black. **1 Kg2 Kg7 2 Kf3 Kf6 3 Ke4 Ke6 4 Kd4 Kd6 5 c4 f6** After 5...Kc6 then 6 Ke5 and invades. **6 b5 h5 7 f4 g5 8 fxg5 fxg5 9 h3 h4 10 g4 Kd7** Or 10...Ke6 11 Kc5 Kd7 12 Kb6 axb5 13 cxb5 Kc8 14 Ka7 Kc7 15 b6+ Kc6 16 a6 and White queens. **11 Kd5 Kc7** 11...Ke7 allows White to queen with 12 bxa6 bxa6 13 Kc6 Kd8 14 Kb7 Kd7 15 c5 etc. **12 Ke6 Kc8 13 Kd6 axb5** 13...Kd8 loses the a-pawn to 14 bxa6 bxa6 15 Kc6 Kc8. **14 cxb5 Kd8 15 a6 bxa6 16 bxa6 Kc8 17 Ke6 Kb8 18 Kf5 Ka7 19 Kxg5 Kxa6 20 Kxh4 Kb7 21 g5** and wins.

White had everything under control; it was so comfortable. With an extra piece for each party things are never so simple.

Now let's look at some of the most basic pawn endings. A mastery of these will enable the reader to solve more involved positions. A good memory is not as important as applying the general principles to the manoeuvres and bearing in mind the consequences of further simplification.

TIP: Try to remember the principles and the ideas behind the solution, not the exact positions. In endings we need to _apply_ our knowledge and experience.

The following position is won comfortably with either player to move.

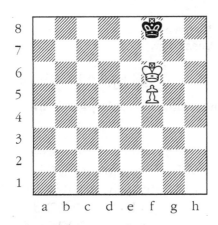

Diagram 2
White's king is in front of his pawn

1 Ke6 Ke8 2 f6 Kf8 3 f7 Kg7 4 Ke7 Kg6 5 f8Q Comfortable enough and with Black to play things are just as routine: 1...Kg8 2 Ke7 followed by advancing the f-pawn.

Imagine the same position with a minor piece each on the board (for instance add a white bishop on b3 and a black one on e8, or say a white knight on h5 and a black knight on d8). Both are drawn and in fact White cannot generally win if Black can defend either the f7 or f8 squares with his piece.

TIP: Exchanging pieces removes useful defenders from the opponent and thus enhances the power of the passed pawn, and the king's ability to shepherd it home.

The a- or h-pawns ('rook's' pawns) yield an important exception. Here White cannot win as his opponent runs out of space and thus has a stalemate defence.

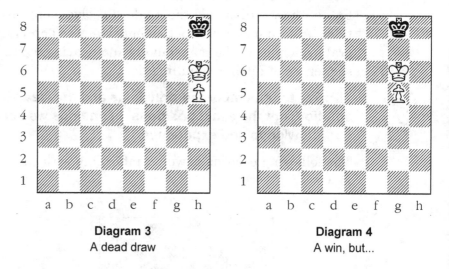

Diagram 3
A dead draw

Diagram 4
A win, but...

From Diagram 3: **1 Kg6 Kg8 2 h6 Kh8 3 h7** stalemate.

TIP: In many endings rook's pawns offer better defensive chances.

In Diagram 4, with a g-pawn, there is a stalemate trap for the unwary. **1 Kh6!** Unfortunate is 1 Kf6?! Kh7! 2 g6+? Kh8! 3 Kf7 and the game ends abruptly as a draw and 3 g7+ Kg8 4 Kg6 is no better. **1...Kh8 2 g6 Kg8 3 g7 Kf7 4 Kh7 Kf6 5 g8Q** It's useful to know that after 1 Kf6?! Kh7! it's not yet too late to win. White has to play 2 Kf7! Kh8 3 Kg6 Kg8 getting back to the starting position where he can then win with 4 Kh6! etc.

The Square

In Diagram 5 White wins because his pawn cannot be caught.

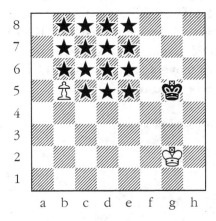

Diagram 5
The black king is too far away

1...Kf5 2 b6 Ke6 3 b7 Kd7 4 b8Q

In the diagram we can mentally construct a square by creating a line from b5 to e5 and to e8 and b8. This is the 'square' of the pawn. If the black king can enter the square then he can catch the pawn. If not, then he can't.

Connected Pawns and Isolated Pawns

Diagram 6
Connected passed pawns are a powerful force

Here Black is within the square of the two connected passed pawns. However, he dare not take the rear pawn as he is then outside the square of the remaining one.

White wins but only by using his king, which is free to support the pawns. **1...Kb6** 1...Kxc4 fails to 2 b6. **2 Kf2 Kc5 3 Ke3 Kb6 4 Kd4 Kb7 5 Kc5 Kc7 6 b6+ Kb7 7 Kb5 Kb8 8 Kc6 Kc8 9 b7+ Kb8 10 c5** Avoiding stalemate and spending a tempo to force Black to move away. **10...Ka7 11 Kc7 Ka6 12 b8Q Ka5 13 Qb3 Ka6 14 Qb6 mate.**

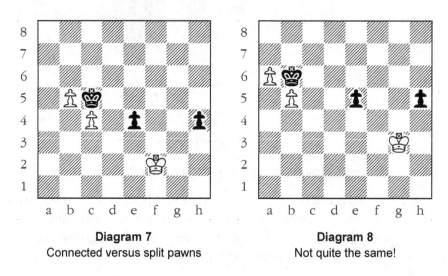

Diagram 7
Connected versus split pawns

Diagram 8
Not quite the same!

In Diagram 7 Black's king is again tied down by the connected passed pawns. However, the white king cannot come to their support as he has problems of his own.

White is in the squares of both black pawns, but not for long! **1 Ke3 h3 2 Kf2** 2 Kxe4 steps out of the square of the h-pawn: 2...h2 3 Kf3 h1Q+. **2...e3+ 3 Kg3 e2 4 Kf2 h2** White simply couldn't cope with the widely spaced passed pawns. However, before reaching a conclusion, let's look at the next example.

Diagram 8 looks similar but now White wins! **1 Kh4 e4** Stopping White from taking the h-pawn as he is then outside the square of the e-pawn. **2 Kg3 Ka7** 2...e3 3 Kf3 changes nothing. **3 Kf4 h4 4 Kxe4 h3 5 Kf3** Now White is inside the square of the remaining pawn! He wins by first eliminating the remaining black pawn and then by supporting his own pawns.

Two unsupported isolated passed pawns, two files apart and on the same rank: win if on the fifth rank but lose if only on the fourth.

 TIP: Play through these last two examples again, concentrating on the king's relation to the squares of the pawns.

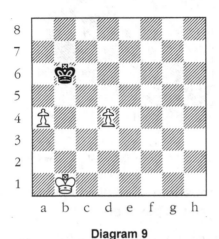

Diagram 9
The white king must help his split pawns

Here the two pawns are exposed. Thus after 1...Ka5 2 d5? fails to 2...Kb6 and Black picks up the d-pawn and holds the game (as the remaining pawn is only a 'rook's' pawn). White would indeed be unable to do anything about this if his king were on the a1-square. However, with the king on b1 he can win.

From the diagram, this can be achieved by answering **1...Ka5** with **2 Kc2! Kxa4 3 Kd3 Kb5 4 Ke4 Kc6 5 Ke5 Kd7 6 Kd5** and White has the 'opposition' (a special type of zugzwang discussed next). **6...Ke7 7 Kc6** and wins.

The Opposition and King Routes

In Diagram 10 White is behind the pawn and Black can draw.

1...Kd7! The only move. **2 d6 Kd8!** Black waits for his opponent to come to the sixth, before opposing the king two squares away on the same file. This is a standard example of taking the 'opposition'. Instead 2...Ke8? immediately allows White to take the 'opposition' with 3 Ke6 and now Black must give way with 3...Kd8 and is squeezed out to the side after 4 d7 Kc7 5 Ke7 and wins. **3 Ke6 Ke8** Black 'faces off' the white king. **4 d7+ Kd8 5 Kd6** and it's stalemate.

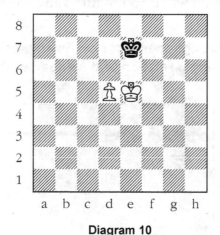

Diagram 10
Using the 'opposition', Black draws

 TIP: The 'opposition' is really a special type of zugzwang commonly seen in pawn endings.

The king that is obliged to move first has to yield ground (it's almost a question of honour between monarchs!) and the other can thus find a way to take up an ideal outpost. When the defender obtains the opposition this enables him to avoid penetration into his camp, whereas when the attacker gains the opposition he is able to make an important breakthrough.

Let's take a look at some practical examples of the opposition.

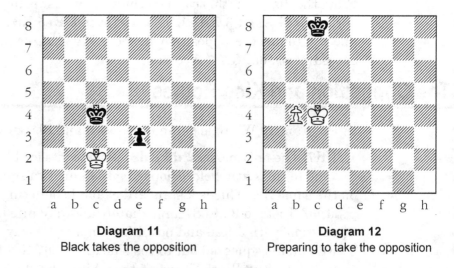

Diagram 11
Black takes the opposition

Diagram 12
Preparing to take the opposition

Diagram 11 is a simple enough looking position but an important one. In Nenarokov-Grigoriev, Moscow 1924, White to play loses as follows: **1 Kc1 Kc3! 2 Kd1 Kd3 3 Ke1 e2** and queens as we have already seen. Black to play has 1...Kd4 meeting 2 Kd1 with 2...Kd3 or 2 Kc1 with 2...Kc3. In either case Black takes the opposition and forces his pawn through.

In Gligoric-Fischer, Yugoslavia 1959 (Diagram 12), Black to play draws by preparing to take the opposition.

Fischer had just exchanged rooks aiming for this position. After the surprising **1...Kb8!** White cannot win. As soon as White's king advances, Black takes the opposition. **2 Kb5** Or 2 Kc5 Kc7! **2...Kb7!** The result is then not in doubt... **3 Ka5 Ka7 4 b5 Kb7 5 b6 Kb8 6 Ka6 Ka8 7 b7+ Kb8 8 Kb6** but take note of Black's play as many of his moves are the only good ones.

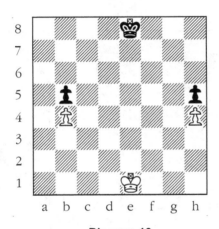

Diagram 13
The 'distant opposition'

The opposition can also play a role when the kings are further apart or even at opposite ends of the board.

It's possible to talk about the 'distant opposition' and other such terms. They all involve the two kings separated by an odd number of squares. An instructive example is this study of Capablanca's. **1 Ke2** White takes the distant opposition. **1...Kf8** Or 1...Ke7 2 Ke3 again taking 'a-not-so-distant' opposition, after which 2...Ke6 3 Ke4 is a more routine opposition. Black to move must give way and allow the white king to penetrate one side or the other. **2 Kd3** Threatening to grab the b-pawn with

Kd4-c5 etc. **2...Ke7** Rushing over to hold the queenside. **3 Ke3!** Again the opposition is taken and thus something has to give. **3...Ke6** If 3...Kd7 then 4 Kf4 going for the kingside or 3...Kf7 4 Kd4 and White wins the b-pawn. **4 Ke4** Maintaining the opposition. Black thus loses a pawn and the game. **4...Kd6 5 Kd4!** A subtle point. 5 Kf5 would allow a counterattack by 5...Kd5. **5...Kc6** Note that now after 5...Ke6 6 Kc5 Kf5 7 Kxb5 Black is too slow. **6 Ke5 Kb7 7 Kd5 Kb6 8 Kd6 Kb7 9 Kc5 Ka6 10 Kc6** and finally the b-pawn is lost. The rest of the analysis is typical of such positions; White cannot win without coming for the h-pawn. **10...Ka7 11 Kxb5 Kb7 12 Kc5 Kc7 13 Kd5 Kb6 14 Ke5 Kb5 15 Kf5 Kxb4 16 Kg5 Kc5 17 Kxh5 Kd6 18 Kg6 Ke7 19 Kg7!** keeping the defending king definitively out of the corner and protecting the route for the passed pawn.

King Routes

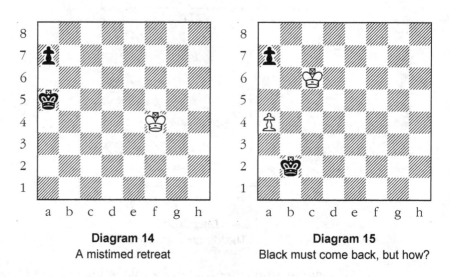

Diagram 14
A mistimed retreat

Diagram 15
Black must come back, but how?

In Berger-Mason, Breslau 1889 (Diagram 14), White to move has to come back as quickly as possible to stop the pawn queening. **1 Ke3!** In the game, White lost after 1 Ke4?? Kb4 2 Kd3 Kb3 3 Kd2 Kb2. **1...Kb4 2 Kd2 Kb3 3 Kc1 Ka2** Or 3...a5 4 Kb1 a4 5 Ka1. **4 Kc2** and draws. So White should have paid more attention as to which route he had in mind to get to the corner. In fact, if White had understood that he should first get to c1 as quickly as possible (to hold-off the black king from playing ...Kb2) then from the diagram the route Ke3-d2-c1 is crucial, and thus 1 Ke3 is called for.

In Diagram 15 White will win the black a-pawn, but if Kxa7 by White is met by ...Kc7 then the draw is assured. **1...Kc3!** 1...Kb3? runs into trouble: 2 a5 Kc4 3 a6 Kd4 4 Kb7 Kc5 5 Kxa7 Kc6 6 Kb8. **2 a5 Kd4!** **3 a6** Nor does 3 Kb7 win due to 3...Kc5 4 Kxa7 Kc6 5 Kb8 Kb5. **3...Ke5 4 Kb7 Kd6 5 Kxa7 Kc7** and Black draws. The route taken by Black's king (b2-c3-d4-e5-d6-c7) is worthy of note – not exactly a straight line, but the only route to draw. Black walked round the houses from b2 to e5 and then to c7 as this avoided being held off by the opposing king.

TIP: In mathematics the shortest route between two points is a straight line. In chess, for king walks there are often several equidistant routes. Always be aware of the possibilities of the indirect route.

In the following example, by creating a threat on one wing Black buys time to race back to the other. Again, as in the previous examples, a slightly indirect route proves to be the best method.

Diagram 16
How to stop the f-pawn?

From Yates-Marshall, Karlovy Vary 1929. Not 1...Kc2 because of 2 f4 etc. but **1...Kb2!** A 'feint', with the threat of advancing the a-pawn, and after... **2 Kxa4 Kc3 3 f4 Kd4** Black is back in the square!

TIP: The square has to be modified for pawns still on their starting block due to the option of moving two ranks forward.

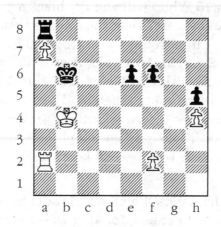

Diagram 17
Can Black hold the pawn ending?

In Flear-Rausis, Gonfreville 1998, my opponent had to decide whether to struggle on in an inferior rook ending or simplify to a pawn ending a pawn up, but with the white king invading his camp. It's hard to imagine but the same theme as in the previous example crops up and decides the game!

This 'feinting' theme was correctly calculated by my opponent who in this position saw that he could simplify and draw. **42...Rxa7 43 Rxa7 Kxa7 44 Kc5 e5 45 Kd5 Kb6 46 Ke6 Kc5 47 Kxf6 Kd5 48 Kg5 Ke4 49 Kxh5 Kf3 50 Kg5 Kxf2 51 Kf5** (see Diagram 18). Does this look familiar, now?

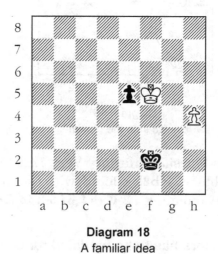

Diagram 18
A familiar idea

Black draws with... **51...Kf3! 52 Kxe5** and a draw was agreed as 52...Kg4 eliminates the last pawn.

This represents an excellent example of an experienced player applying his knowledge to solving a practical problem.

The Outside Passed Pawn

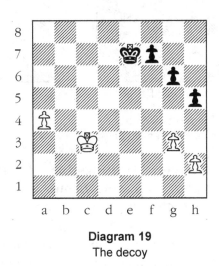

Diagram 19
The decoy

In the case of opposing majorities, the pawn that is passed and furthest away from the bulk of the action is called an outside passed pawn. An important trump, it obliges the opposing king to expend several crucial tempo to deal with the pest. Naturally in the meantime White will cause havoc on the other wing, as shown in this example from Fischer-Larsen, Denver 1971.

1 Kd4 Kd6 2 a5 f6 Attempting to keep White out of the e5-square. Instead 2...Kc6 leads to the loss of the whole kingside: 3 Ke5 Kb5 4 Kf6 Kxa5 5 h4 Kb5 6 Kxf7 Kc5 7 Kxg6. **3 a6 Kc6 4 a7 Kb7 5 Kd5 h4 6 Ke6!** Not making the mistake of giving Black a protected passed pawn by taking on h4. **6...f5 7 Kf6 Kxa7 8 Kxg6 hxg3 9 hxg3** Only one pawn each, but Black's king is too far away. **9...Kb7 10 Kxf5 Kc7 11 Kf6 Kd7 12 Kf7 Kd6 13 g4** White just keeps pushing to victory.

Possession of the outside passed pawn was a decisive factor.

 TIP: The outside passed pawn acts as a decoy, gaining time whilst forcing the opposing king far away from the other wing.

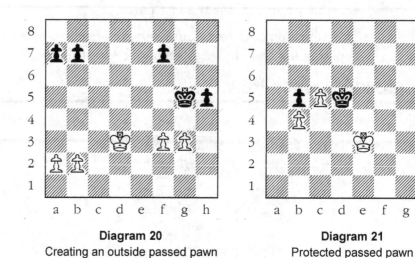

Diagram 20
Creating an outside passed pawn

Diagram 21
Protected passed pawn

In Gheorghiu-Gligoric, Hastings 1964 (Diagram 20), Black to move has the plan of creating an outside passed pawn. **1...f5! 2 Ke3** After 2 Ke2 f4 the h-pawn is more dangerous than the white f-pawn. **2...f4+! 3 Kf2** Or 3 gxf4+ Kf5 4 Kf2 Kxf4 5 Kg2 b5 with an even better version of the game continuation. **3...b5** Preparing the switch to the queenside, by moving the b-pawn closer to the queening square. **4 Kg2 b4 5 Kf2 fxg3+ 6 Kxg3 h4+ 7 Kh3 Kf4 8 Kxh4 Kxf3** Material is equal but White's king is further away. **9 Kg5 Ke3 10 Kf5 Kd3 11 Ke5 Kc2 12 Kd5 Kxb2 13 Kc5 a5 14 Kb5 Kxa2 15 Kxa5 b3** The decoy enabled Gligoric to obtain a head-start in the queenside race.

In Diagram 21 Black has the outside passed pawn, but this is overshadowed by the importance of White's protected passed pawn. Black can do nothing but sit and watch while his opponent picks off the black h-pawn and marches across the board to win on the queenside. **1 Kf3 Ke5** 1...Kc4 2 c6 etc. **2 Kg3 Kf5 3 Kh4 Ke5** 3...Kg6 4 c6 etc. **4 Kxh5 Kd5 5 Kg4 Ke6 6 Kf4 Kf6 7 Ke4 Ke6 8 Kd4 Ke7 9 Kd5 Kd7 10 c6+ Kc7 11 Kc5** and with the fall of the b-pawn the win is clear.

TIP: An outside passed pawn gains time but a protected passed pawn can be a permanent advantage.

Diagram 22 shows a difficult example from a game Kushnir-Sulim, USSR 1976, which can only be resolved by analysis. White has an outside passed pawn and Black has a protected passed pawn, but this can be undermined.

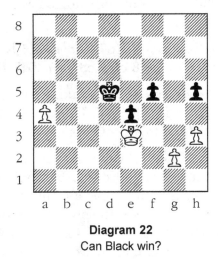

Diagram 22
Can Black win?

1...f4+! The only way, forcing a race. Alternatives are lacking, for instance 1...Kc4 2 g4! liquidates all of Black's kingside pawns: 2...hxg4 3 hxg4 fxg4 4 Kxe4 and draws. **2 Kxf4 Kd4 3 a5 e3 4 a6 e2 5 a7 e1Q 6 a8Q** Before provoking the race, the queen ending needed to be calculated. Black is indeed winning and followed up with **6...Qe5+ 7 Kf3 Qe3 mate**.

TIP: Consideration of various features of the pawn structure should help the player decide if entering a race is wise or simply unnecessary.

More Advanced Ideas

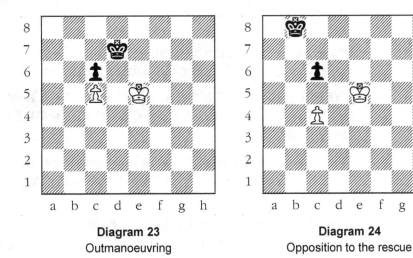

Diagram 23
Outmanoeuvring

Diagram 24
Opposition to the rescue

In Diagram 23 a series of zugzwangs force Black to give ground until the c-pawn falls.

1 Kf6 Kd8 2 Ke6 Kc7 3 Ke7 Kc8 4 Kd6 Kb7 5 Kd7 Kb8 6 Kxc6 Kc8 7 Kb6 Kb8 8 c6 Kc8 9 c7 Kd7 10 Kb7 and wins.

In Diagram 24 Black draws by taking the opposition at the moment his pawn is captured. This can be done if the pawn is on the fifth, but not to any effect if on the sixth.

1...c5! 1...Kc7 2 c5 Kd7 3 Kf6 etc. as in the previous diagram or 1...Kb7 2 c5 Ka6 3 Ke6 (3 Kd6?? Kb5 would be embarrassing, a special double-zugzwang called a trébuchet, whoever is to move loses!) 3...Ka5 (3...Kb5 4 Kd6 now White wins) 4 Kd7 Kb5 5 Kd6. **2 Kd5 Kb7! 3 Kxc5 Kc7! 4 Kb5 Kb7 5 c5 Kc7 6 c6 Kc8!** and draws. A nice technical trick that is well worth knowing.

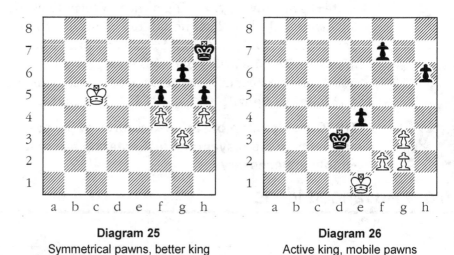

Diagram 25
Symmetrical pawns, better king

Diagram 26
Active king, mobile pawns

The more active king was enough to win in Gurgenidze-Averbakh, USSR Championship 1961 (Diagram 25).

1 Kd5 Kg7 2 Ke6 Kh6 3 Kf6 Kh7 4 Kf7 Kh6 5 Kg8 Black is forced to play the suicidal **5...g5 6 hxg5+ Kg6 7 Kh8** and is thus totally lost.

A better king with mobile pawns enabled Black, in Marshall-Nimzowitsch, Berlin 1928 (Diagram 26), to break up and expose White's pawns.

1...h5 Fixing the pawns **2 Kd1 e3 3 fxe3** After 3 f3 e2+ 4 Ke1 Ke3 5 g4 hxg4 6 fxg4 f6 White has no alternative but to play 7 g5 fxg5 8 g4 when 8...Kf3 wins easily. **3...Kxe3 4 Ke1 Ke4 5 Kf2 Kf5 6 Kf3 Kg5** Black has prudently kept back a reserve tempo with his f-pawn in order to force zugzwang and thus White's g4-square and g3-pawn are impossible to defend. **7 Ke3 Kg4 8 Kf2 f6! 9 Kf1 Kxg3 10 Kg1 h4 11 Kf1 h3 12 Kg1** Or 12 gxh3 Kxh3 13 Kf2 Kg4 14 Ke3 f5 15 Kf2 Kf4 and wins by 16 Kg2 Ke3 17 Kf1 f4 18 Ke1 f3 19 Kf1 f2. **12...Kg4!** Avoiding stalemate and winning as in the previous note. **13 Kh2 hxg2 14 Kxg2 f5 15 Kf2 Kf4 16 Ke2 Kg3** and so on.

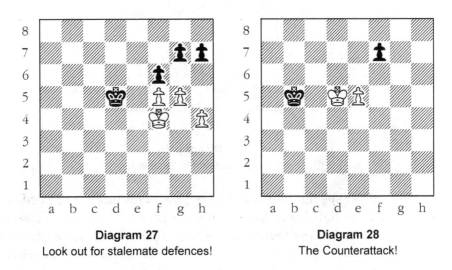

Diagram 27
Look out for stalemate defences!

Diagram 28
The Counterattack!

In Diagram 27 stalemate looks out of the question. Black is gradually outmanoeuvring the white king who is being pushed away from his f-pawn.

1 Kg4! In the game Chigorin-Tarrasch, Ostend 1906, White lost tamely with 1 gxf6? gxf6 2 Kg4 Ke4 3 Kh3 (3 Kh5 fails to 3...Kxf5 4 Kh6 Kg4 5 Kxh7 Kh5! – a neat resource; the h-pawn is stymied and the f-pawn will advance) 3...Kf4! and he loses both pawns. **1...Ke4 2 g6 h6** After 2...hxg6 White can obtain counterplay with 3 fxg6 f5+ 4 Kg5 f4 5 h5 f3 6 h6. **3 Kh5** and now if 3...Kxf5 it's stalemate!

A clever resource which was missed by one of the world's leading players, but if you stay alert to such possibilities, games can be saved at the last moment!

In Panno-Silva Nazzari, Argentina 1975 (Diagram 28), Black found a counterattacking defence that draws neatly.

1...Kb4! The natural 1...Kb6? loses time after 2 Kd6 and the game after the further 2...Kb7 3 Ke7. **2 Kd6 Kc4 3 Ke7 Kd5**

TIP: Even in pawn endings, a timely counterattack can be a better option than passive defence.

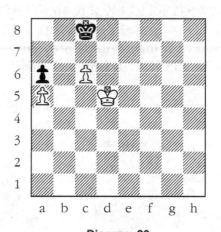

Diagram 29
Manoeuvring to force entry

A special feature of pure pawn endings is the need sometimes to indulge in king walks in order to lose time. This position is one of my favourite training tools. As a young player I was impressed with the solution to this problem, and excited that a few months later I almost had the same position in a game!

How can White win? If 1 Kd6 then 1...Kd8 or if 2 Kc5 then 2...Kc7 and in either case Black takes the opposition, stopping any white penetration for the moment. However, what happens if it is Black to play? 1...Kc7 loses to 2 Kc5 and 1...Kd8 to 2 Kd6. So the solution is to find a way to pass the move to Black.

1 Kc4! What's this? The king is going backwards! **1...Kd8 2 Kd4!** Now it's sideways. **2...Kc8 3 Kd5** Changed his mind, you may think. However we now have *the same position with Black to play*. **3...Kd8** Equally hopeless is 3...Kc7 4 Kc5 Kc8 5 Kb6 Kb8 6 Kxa6. **4 Kd6 Kc8 5 c7 Kb7 6 Kd7 Ka7** It's never too late to make a mistake, so... **7 Kc6!** Better than 7 c8Q with stalemate! **7...Ka8 8 c8Q+ Ka7 9 Qb7 mate**.

Note: The White walk Kd5-c4-d4-d5 is called triangulation. White can thus lose a tempo and induce zugzwang because Black lacks the equivalent manoeuvring space.

Here is a practical example from the highest level.

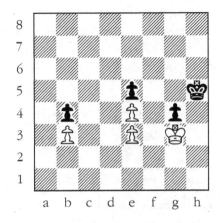

Diagram 30
Can Black invade the white camp?

Black has a passed pawn in Botvinnik-Smyslov, World Championship match 1958, and thus a clear advantage. However, as entry into the white camp is blocked for the present, some instructive manoeuvring is required to force a way through.

1 Kg2 Kh4 2 Kh2 g3+ 3 Kg1 Rather than 3 Kg2? Kg4 and White is forced to give way. **3...Kg5!** 3...Kg4 gets nowhere as 4 Kg2 takes the opposition and holds for the present. **4 Kh1 Kh5! 5 Kg1 Kh4!** Black's triangulates. As White has only limited manoeuvring space available, he is forced to a 'mined' square. **6 Kh1** Or 6 Kg2 Kg4 7 Kg1 Kf3 etc. **6...Kh3 7 Kg1 g2 8 Kf2 Kh2** and queens.

TIP: Passing the move in all endings is a useful weapon. In pawn endings if a reserve pawn move is not available, triangulation sometimes does the trick.

Try it Yourself

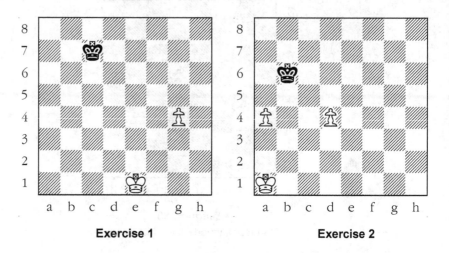

Exercise 1   Exercise 2

Exercise 1: Can you find a path to victory?

Exercise 2: Black to play is two pawns down, but can he draw?

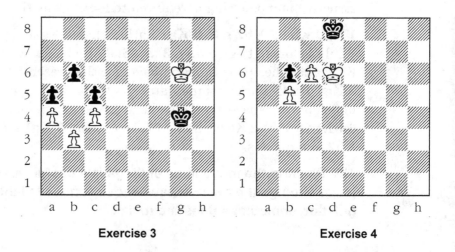

Exercise 3   Exercise 4

Exercise 3: White to play gets to the queenside only just before Black. Is this enough to win?

Exercise 4: White has an extra pawn, but can he win?

Summary

Zugzwang and the opposition are common features.

An extra pawn is usually enough to win.

Protected passed pawns and outside passed pawns are frequently decisive.

A slightly better king can be enough to obtain the full point.

Chapter Four

Knight Endgames

- ■ Converting an Extra Pawn

- ■ Other Types of Advantage

- ■ Endings with Reduced Material

- ■ Try it Yourself

Endings with just knights, kings and pawns are considered the closest in character to pure pawn endings. This is perhaps the most striking in the case of an extra pawn for one side and no counterplay for the other, as again this is almost always decisive. With many pawns for each player the defence can be equally as hopeless, but in examples with very few pawns remaining there is naturally the extra defensive option of sacrificing the knight for the remaining opposing pawns.

NOTE: The ending of king and knight against lone king is drawn.

Knights are essentially short-range pieces that have the characteristic of changing the colour of their square each time they move. This means they are the only chess piece that, on their own, cannot triangulate, so here again it's the kings that do the dodging and weaving. In compensation, they are the only pieces that can leap over other pieces or pawns.

Converting an Extra Pawn

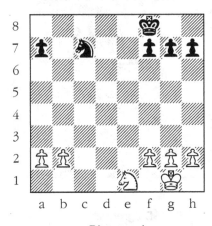

Diagram 1
A clear extra pawn

The step-by-step winning plan is fairly logical: Centralising the king and knight, then supporting the pawn majority to create a passed pawn, which advances towards the queening square and/or is sacrificed as a decoy to gain time for invasion on the opposite wing.

1 Kf1 Ke7 2 Ke2 Kd6 3 Kd3 Kc5 Stopping White's queenside

for the moment. **4 Nc2 Nd5 5 g3 a5 6 b3 f5 7 a3 g6 8 b4+!**
White is quite willing to simplify to a pawn ending where his
king is much closer to the kingside. **8...axb4 9 axb4+ Kd6** After studying the previous chapter you probably realise that
9...Nxb4+ loses but here's a sample line: 10 Nxb4 Kxb4 11 Kd4
Kb3 12 f4 Kc2 13 Ke5 Kd3 14 Kf6 Ke4 15 Kg7 Kf3 16 Kxh7 Kg2
17 Kxg6 Kxh2 18 Kxf5 Kxg3 19 Kg5 etc. **10 Kd4 Nc7 11 f4
Nb5+ 12 Kc4 Nc7 13 Ne3** White has no need to go into the
complications following 13 b5 Nxb5 14 Kxb5 Kd5 15 Ne1 Ke4.
13...Kc6 14 Kd4 Kd6 15 Nc4+ Offering a difficult choice for
Black who must allow the white king to advance. **15...Kc6**
15...Ke6 allows 16 Kc5 or even 16 Ne5 Kd6 17 Nf7+ Ke7 18 Ng5
h6 19 Nf3 Kf6 20 Kc5. **16 Ke5 Kb5 17 Ne3 Na6** Black loses
further time as 17...Kxb4 18 Nd5+ again leads to a winning
pawn ending. **18 Nd5 Kc4 19 Nf6 h5 20 Nd5 Nb8 21 Ne7
Kxb4 22 Nxg6** and White mops up the kingside.

In the following example White has no passed pawns but with
knights he has excellent winning chances.

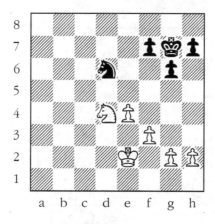

Diagram 2
All the pawns on one wing

This type of ending occurs time and again in practical play: one
player wins a pawn but the other succeeds in exchanging off all
the pawns on one wing.

The same pawn structure but without pieces is a clear win,
with knights White is probably winning. However, if we instead
gave each side a bishop of either colour, or a rook (say rooks on
a7 and d6) or indeed a queen (on a7 and d6) then in each case a

draw would be the most likely result.

TIP: Knight endings are the closest in character to pure pawn endings.

Let's see how White wins against passive defence.

1...Kf6 2 g3 Ke5 3 Nc6+ Ke6 4 Ke3 Kd7 5 Nd4 f6 6 f4 Ke7 7 h4 Gradually White enhances his space advantage and restricts the black knight. **7...Nf7 8 g4 Kd7 9 Kd3 Ke7 10 Kc4 Kd6 11 g5** Creating a passed pawn after all! **11...fxg5 12 hxg5 Ke7 13 e5 Nd8 14 Kd5 Nf7 15 Nc6+ Ke8 16 e6 Nh8 17 Ke5 Kf8 18 Kf6** and Black is squeezed into submission.

Let's check how a more active defence fares.

4...f5 Instead of 4...Kd7. **5 Nd4+ Kf6 6 exf5 gxf5 7 Kf4 Kg6 8 Ke5 Nf7+ 9 Ke6 Nd8+ 10 Ke7 Nb7 11 Ne6 Na5 12 Nf4+ Kg5 13 h4+ Kh6 14 Kf6** and the f-pawn and all hope are lost.

These are sample lines and not exhaustive, which is why I covered myself by claiming that White *probably* wins!

TIP: The black knight proves to be an ineffective defender when White can centralise his knight and use his king and pawns to take away useful squares from the enemy piece.

Other Types of Advantage

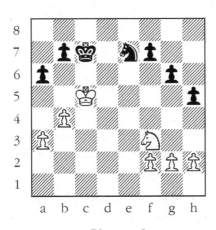

Diagram 3
A space advantage

In Botvinnik-Kholmov, Moscow 1969, simply having the more advanced king seems rather a modest advantage, particularly as Black is threatening to push it back with ...b7-b6+. However, White can create a few chinks in the black armour by probing away at some sensitive points.

1 Ng5 f6 2 Nh7 f5 3 h4 Fixing the g6-pawn as a static weakness. **3...f4 4 Nf8 b6+** Black is in no mood to spend the rest of the game with his knight passively defending the g6-pawn! **5 Kd4 Nf5+ 6 Ke4 Nxh4 7 Ne6+ Kc6 8 Nxf4 Kb5** Activating the king as 8...g5 fails to 9 g3! gxf4 10 gxh4 Kb5 11 Kxf4 Ka4 12 Kg5 and White wins the race. **9 g3** But now Black loses the g6-pawn. **9...Nf5 10 Nxg6 Nh6 11 Ne5 Ka4 12 Nc4 Kb3** 12...b5 wins back the pawn, but after 13 Ne5 Kxa3 14 Nc6! the queenside is stymied and White can advance on the king's wing at leisure. **13 Nxb6 Kxa3 14 Nd5 Kb3 15 f4 Kc4 16 Nc7 Kxb4 17 Nxa6+** Black resigned as the f-pawn will cost him his knight, and the g-pawn, after queening, will cost him the whole game.

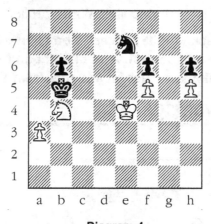

Diagram 4
Knight sacrifices

Knight sacrifices to queen pawns or to invade the opposing camp are not unusual. I was rather proud of the following effort a quarter of a century ago, in Flear-Gould, Leicester 1974!

49 Nd5 Ng8 50 Nxb6! Eliminating Black's last queenside pawn and preparing a decisive entry via the d5-square. **50...Kxb6 51 Kd5 Ne7+ 52 Ke6 Nc6 53 Kxf6 Kc7 54 Kg7 Nd4 55 f6 Kd7 56 Kxh6 Ke6 57 Kg6 Nf5 58 f7 Ne7+ 59 Kg7 Nf5+ 60 Kf8 Nh6** Winning the f-pawn, but the a- and h-pawns are too far apart for the black pieces to stop. **61 a4 Nxf7 62 a5**

Ne5 63 a6 Nd7+ 64 Kg7 Nf6 65 a7 Ne8+ 66 Kf8 Nc7 67 h6
Kf6 68 h7 Ne6+ 69 Kg8 1-0

See Chapter One, Diagram 10 for an example of a thematic
knight sacrifice to immediately promote a pawn.

As in pawn endings far distant passed pawns are useful weapons. Either the knight or king is obliged to deal with the threat
and is kept away from play on the other wing.

**TIP: If it is the knight holding the pawn, unlike the king, it
cannot capture the pawn on its own.**

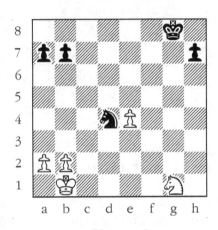

Diagram 5
The outside passed pawn is more dangerous with knights

In the game, Lasker-Nimzowitsch, Zurich 1934, Black's plan is
to centralise his pieces, tie down the knight to the h-pawn and
create play on the queenside. This in turn leads to the white
king being distracted to the queen's wing and allowing a final
run to capture White's passive knight.

**1...Kf7 2 Kc1 Kf6 3 Kd2 Ke5 4 Ke3 h5 5 a3 a5 6 Nh3 Nc2+ 7
Kd3 Ne1+ 8 Ke2 Ng2 9 Kf3 Nh4+ 10 Ke3 Ng6** Nimzowitsch
is seeking to establish his knight on e5. **11 Ng5 Kf6 12 Nh7+
Ke7 13 Ng5 Ne5 14 Kd4 Kd6 15 Nh3 a4 16 Nf4 h4 17 Nh3
b6 18 Nf4 b5 19 Nh3 Nc6+ 20 Ke3 Kc5 21 Kd3 b4** Exchanging pawns in order to loosen the defences. Black's main problem is that with so few pawns remaining he has to be careful
about White sacrificing his knight for the remainder. **22 axb4+
Kxb4 23 Kc2 Nd4+ 24 Kb1 Ne6 25 Ka2 Kc4 26 Ka3 Kd4 27
Kxa4 Kxe4 28 b4 Kf3 29 b5 Kg2** The knight is lost and

Black's knight will handle the b-pawn. One pawn is just enough to win!

This leads us on to a few positions with very limited material.

Endings with Very Little Material

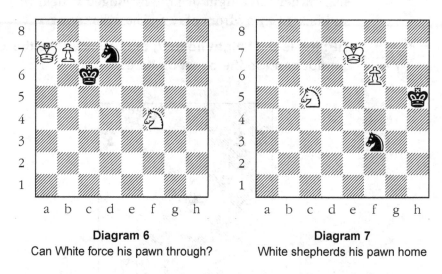

Diagram 6
Can White force his pawn through?

Diagram 7
White shepherds his pawn home

In Diagram 6 White has to attack the opposing knight with his own in order to prise it away from its defence of the b8-square.

1 Ne6 Kd5 2 Nf8 Ne5 Clearly 2...Nxf8 3 b8Q gives White what he wants. **3 Ka8** Avoiding the fork, an important aspect of knight endings which would occur after 3 b8Q Nc6+. **3...Nc6 4 Nd7 Ke6 5 Nb6** 5 Nb8? throws away the win after 5...Na5 followed by ...Nxb7. **5...Kd6 6 Nc8+ Kc7 7 Na7 Nb8** A desperate blockade that is immediately broken. **8 Nb5+** and wins.

In fact as soon as the pawn, supported by his king, reaches the seventh rank there is rarely a defence.

Diagram 7 illustrates another battle to control the queening square. White wants to advance his pawn in safety, carefully avoiding forks and annoying checks.

1 Nd3 Covering the e5-square which Black can use to save himself after 1 f7? Ne5 2 f8Q Ng6+. **1...Ng5 2 Nf4+ Kg4 3 Ne6** Dislodging the knight, but again Black uses a fork to avoid the f-pawn's advance. **3...Nf3 4 Kd6!** This time covering the e5-square with the king. The pawn is finally ready to advance. Of

course 4 f7? still fails to 4...Ne5 5 f8Q Ng6+. **4...Nh4 5 f7 Ng6 6
Nc7** Re-routing to dislodge the black knight from its new defensive outpost. **6...Kg5** Or in the case of 6...Kf5 then 7 Nd5
Kg5 8 Ke6 Nf8+ 9 Ke7 Ng6+ 10 Ke8 Kh6 11 Ne7 does the trick.
**7 Ke6 Kh6 8 Kf6 Kh7 9 Ne6 Kh6 10 Nf4 Nf8 11 Ke7 Nh7 12
Nd5 Kg7 13 Nf6** and finally the way is clear for the pawn to
advance.

There are occasionally chances to hold. In the next example the
black king cannot get in front of the pawn but instead finds its
way *behind the pawn*, supporting the knight in an active defence.

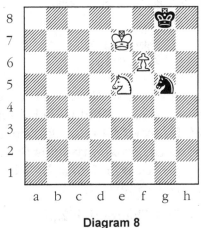

Diagram 8
A defensive resource

Black has to move his king, as he dare not move his knight and
thus allow the pawn to advance.

1...Kh7 1...Nh7? loses as we have already seen: 2 f7+ Kg7 3
Nd7 Kg6 4 Nf6 etc. **2 Nc4** 2 Nf3? fails to a fork: 2...Nxf3 3 f7
Ne5 4 f8Q Ng6+. **2...Kg6 3 Nd6** Threatening 3 Ne4 Nf3
(3...Nxe4 4 f7 wins) 4 f7 so Black frees the g6-square to prepare
the customary defensive fork. **3...Kh5! 4 Ne4 Nf3 5 Ke6** Covering e5. Again 5 f7 Ne5 is an immediate draw and 5 Nc5 Kg4! 6
Ne6 Ne5 7 Nd4 Kf4 8 Ke6 Ke4 neatly illustrates an active defence; Black holds on to the e5-square with his king behind the
pawn. The knight cannot then be dislodged with 9 Nc6 in view
of 9...Nxc6 10 f7 Nd8+. **5...Kg6** Now White advances but Black
harasses him sufficiently to hold the game. **6 f7 Nd4+ 7 Ke7
Nf5+ 8 Ke8 Ng7+ 9 Kf8 Nf5!** Repeating the threat of 10...Nh6

10 Ke8 Ng7+ and White cannot profitably avoid the draw by repetition.

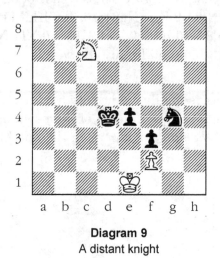

Diagram 9
A distant knight

With only two pawns against one on the same front, White should hold easily if his knight were helping out. In the game, Goldenov-Kan, Moscow 1946, Black tried an interesting winning try based on the proximity of his f-pawn to the queening square and the practical difficulty for White of getting his knight back to base camp.

1...e3! 2 fxe3+ Ke4 The routine 2...Kxe3 3 Nd5+ Ke4 4 Nc3+ Kf4 5 Nd1 is drawn. **3 Kf1 Nxe3+ 4 Kf2 Nd1+ 5 Ke1?** A natural move that proves to be bad. Instead 5 Kg3! Ke3 6 Nd5+ Ke2 7 Nf4+ draws comfortably. **5...f2+ 6 Ke2 Kf4 0-1** White has no reasonable defence to the plan of 7...Kg3 followed by 8...Kg2 or 8...Ne3.

TIP: When defending don't stray too far with your knight.

In Diagram 10 White blockades the passed pawn with both his king and knight. There are only two Black pawns remaining and White would be keen to exchange his knight for the pair. However, despite these substantial technical difficulties Black was able to win in the game Chernikov-Chekhover, Leningrad 1948.

Firstly Black gradually pushes back the defending pieces.

Diagram 10
An extra passed pawn

1...Ke5 2 Nd2 Nf5+ 3 Ke2 e3 4 Nf3+ Kf4 5 Ne1 Ke4 Preparing 6...Nd4+ and avoiding annoying defensive checks. **6 Kf1 Nd4 7 Kg2 Ne2 8 Nf3 Kd3 9 Ne5+ Kd4** More precise than 9...Kc3? 10 Kf3 Kd2 11 Nc4+ etc. **10 Nf3+ Kc3 11 Ne5** 11 Kf1 is perhaps a tougher defence but Black combines threats with the e-pawn and a stroll across to capture White's h-pawn: 11...Nf4 12 Ke1 Kd3 13 Ne5+ Ke4 14 Nc4 Kf3 15 Ne5+ Kg2 16 h4 h5 17 Nc4 e2 18 Nd6 (or 18 Ne5 Kg3 and ...Kxh4 with a clear win) 18...Kf3 and the e-pawn cannot be stopped. **11...Nf4+ 12 Kf3 e2 13 Kf2 Nd3+** Correctly calculating the pawn ending. **14 Nxd3** 14 Kxe2 Nxe5 15 Ke3 Ng6 16 Ke4 Kd2 17 Kf5 Ke3 18 Kf6 Kf3 19 Kg7 Nf8! 20 Kxf8 h5 and Black wins. **14...Kxd3 15 Ke1 Ke3 16 h4** 16 h3 is met by 16...h5! 17 h4 Kf3. **16...h6!** Timing his pawn move to oblige, by zugzwang, the white king to move away. **17 h5 Kf3** and White is finished.

Try it Yourself

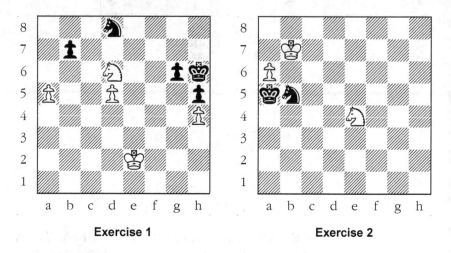

Exercise 1   Exercise 2

Exercise 1: What is the clearest winning method for White?

Exercise 2: Black to play is in zugzwang. After **1...Kb4** How does White win quickly?

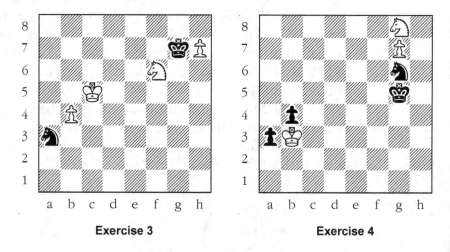

Exercise 3   Exercise 4

Exercise 3: How should White continue?

Exercise 4: White to move. What result?

Summary

Play in knight endings is often similar to that of pawn endings.

Knights are poor defenders if play is on a wide front.

A knight on its own cannot triangulate.

The winning technique usually involves taking away useful squares from the opponent's knight.

Chapter Five

Bishops of the Same Colour

- Good and Bad Bishops

- Converting Extra Material

- The Last Pawn

- More Advanced Ideas

- Try it Yourself

With endgames featuring bishops of the same colour, there are a number of notable differences from the previous chapter on knights.

On the positive side: Bishops are long-range pieces which can have an influence on both sides of the board at the same time and have the characteristic of being able to lose a move and so create zugzwangs.

On the negative side: They operate uniquely on one predetermined colour.

Advantageous knight endings are often easier to win than bishop endings, especially with limited material. One of the reasons can be understood by studying the next diagram. This position illustrates an important drawing possibility that crops up time and again in this chapter. The term 'wrong rook's pawn' refers to this type of position.

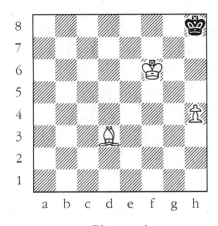

Diagram 1
A draw as the black king is in the corner

This is an important position for the evaluation of many bishop endings. Not only is king and bishop against king always a draw but the position in the diagram is too!

The black king shuffles backwards and forwards, never venturing away from the corner. White cannot force him away and if he gets too close then stalemate occurs.

1 h5 Kg8 2 h6 Kh8 3 Kg6 Kg8 4 Bc4+ Kh8 5 h7 The result is not the same if the black king can be prevented from reaching the corner or if White's bishop controls the queening square.

TIP: Even with many more pieces and pawns on the board, look out for the possibility of the inferior side heading for this position.

Good and Bad Bishops

Even with more material, if the king of the attacking side cannot enter the opposing camp a win may be impossible, as the bishop can only attack pawns and squares of one colour. Potential weaknesses on the other colour squares may be out of reach.

In a position with a number of blocked pawns, bishops are often informally regarded as 'good' and 'bad' ones. In general a bad bishop is one that has its sphere of influence significantly restricted by its own pawns.

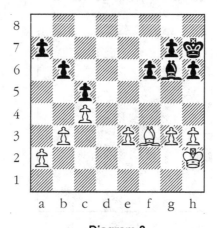

Diagram 2
White has an inferior pawn structure

In the game Smyslov-Keres, Moscow 1951, both bishops seem to enjoy open diagonals for the present, but White's pawns will be a source of problems in the play that follows. His queenside is placed on the same-coloured squares as the bishop and his kingside pawns are split.

 NOTE: Pawns that are placed on the same colour as the bishops are exposed to attack and can restrict the bishop's scope for action.

1...Bb1 2 a3 a5! Fixing the b-pawn on b3 and threatening 3...Bc2. **3 Bd1** White's bishop is thus forced into passive mode;

if it ever moves from here then ...Bc2 picks up at least a pawn. **3...Kg6** The kings are naturally centralised. White aims to avoid a black invasion via e4 and d3. **4 Kg2 Kf5 5 Kf3 Ke5** Another problem for White is that his bishop has no moves, so he will soon be in zugzwang! **6 a4 g5 7 Ke2 Bf5!** Forcing White to further place his pawns on light squares. **8 g4** The pawn ending is lost after 8 h4 Bg4+ 9 Kd2 Bxd1 10 Kxd1 Ke4 11 Ke2 g4 12 h5 f5 etc. **8...Bb1 9 Kf3 f5!** Giving White a difficult choice. **10 gxf5** After 10 Ke2 Be4 11 Kf2 f4 12 exf4+ Kxf4 White is in zugzwang and is forced to allow the black king to invade to decisive effect. With all his pawns on light squares, White is very weak on the dark squares. **10...Kxf5 11 Kf2 Be4 12 Kg3 Kg6** Preparing the h-pawn's advance. **13 Kf2 h5 14 Kg3 h4+** Fixing the h-pawn to h3, another target. Now with weak points on both wings to attack, Black strolls through the centre. **15 Kf2 Bf5 16 Kg2 Kf6 17 Kh2 Ke6!** Losing a move in order to time the invasion for when White's king is furthest away. **18 Kg2 Ke5 19 Kh2 Bb1 20 Kg2 Ke4 21 Kf2 Kd3 22 Kf3 Kd2 23 Be2 Bf5** White resigned as the last gasp try for activity with 24 e4 is refuted by 24...Bxe4+ 25 Kxe4 Kxe2 26 Kf5 Kf3 27 Kxg5 Kg3. An excellent example of a 'good' bishop against a 'bad' counterpart.

TIP: Even when there are more pieces on the board, take into account the pawn structure and bear in mind which bishops may later become 'bad' ones.

The next example is also instructive

Diagram 3
Who is better?

In the game Averbakh-Veresov, Moscow 1947, Black has a passed pawn and a well-centralised king. However, these are not going anywhere and meanwhile he has several pawns on light squares exposed to attack by White's bishop. White has an ace up his sleeve in the form of a queenside majority.

1 h4! Fixing the kingside pawns on light squares. **1...Bd7 2 Bf1 a5 3 Bg2 Bc6** After 3...Bf5 White can temporise with 4 Bh1! immediately putting Black into zugzwang. **4 Bh3** Seeking to create further problems by coming round the back. **4...b5** Exchanging a pair of pawns. Waiting doesn't help: 4...Ba8 5 Bd7 Bb7 6 b4 axb4 7 axb4 Ba8 8 c5 (creating a passed pawn to distract Black from his kingside pawns) 8...bxc5 9 bxc5 Kd5 10 Be8 g5 (leaving White with only doubled pawns) 11 hxg5 Kxc5 12 Bg6! (preferring the e-pawn as the h-pawn can be captured later) 12...Bd5 13 Bxe4 Bg8 14 Kf4 Kd6 15 Kf5 Ke7 16 Kg6 Kf8 17 Kf6! (not falling for 17 Kxh5? Kg7 and the black king cannot be shifted from g7) and White wins by pushing his pawn to g7 and taking control of the g8-square. **5 cxb5 Bxb5 6 Bc8 Bc6 7 b4 axb4 8 axb4 Bb5 9 Bb7 g5** Exchanging a pair of pawns to make White's task more difficult. Instead 9...Bd3 fails to the plan of pushing the b-pawn: 10 Bc6 Kf5 11 b5 Kg4 12 b6 Ba6 13 Kf2 e3+ 14 Kg2 winning in view of the threats of b6-b7 and even Bd7 mate! **10 Bxe4 gxh4 11 gxh4 Ba4** There are only two white pawns remaining and one is the 'wrong rook's pawn' but White still wins. An important factor is that Black's remaining pawn is stuck on a light square! **12 Bg6 Bd1 13 b5 Kd5 14 Kf4 Kc5 15 Kg5 Be2 16 Be8** A clever zugzwang move, forcing Black farther away with his king. **16...Kb6 17 Bxh5 Bxb5 18 Bg4 Be8** White must now shield the remaining pawn from the bishop. **19 Bf5 Kc7 20 Bg6 Kd8 21 Kf6!** and wins as the pawn slips through!

A bad bishop can make winning with extra material a difficult task.

The game Flear-Lodhi, London 1987 (Diagram 4), continued **37...Kg8 38 Bd2 Kf7 39 Kf1 Ke8 40 Ke2 Be7 41 Be1 Kd7 42 Kd3 Kc6 43 b4?** A poor move which makes the draw even clearer, but after 43 Kc4 Bd8 44 b4 Be7 45 a4 Bd8 46 b5+ axb5+ 47 axb5+ Kb6 White cannot make progress. For instance, the continuation 48 Bf2+ Kb7 49 b6 Kc6 50 Kb4 Be7+ (50...Bxb6 51 Bxb6 Kxb6 52 Kc4 Kc6 is also drawn) 51 Ka5 Kb7

52 Kb5 Bd8 is instructive. White's bishop is always tied to the h4-pawn and his king cannot enter the black camp. **43...Kb5 44 a3 Bd8 45 Bf2 Be7 46 Kc3 a5 47 bxa5 Bxa3 48 Kd3 Kxa5 49 Kc4 Be7** Drawing. White's bishop was bad and his king never had a chance to invade and pressurise the black kingside.

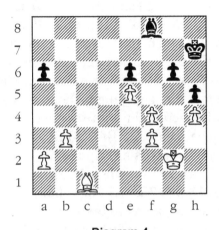

Diagram 4
White has two extra pawns but cannot win

Converting Extra Material

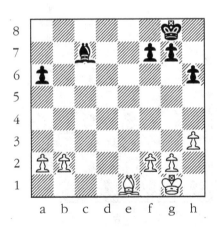

Diagram 5
White has an extra pawn

With a clear extra pawn in an open position the win is similar to that with knights.

White centralises, creates a passed pawn and uses it to create threats or as a decoy on the queenside, enabling him to invade with his king and capture some kingside pawns.

1 Kf1 Kf8 2 Ke2 Ke8 3 Kd3 Kd7 4 Kc4 An excellent square to prepare the advance of the queenside. **4...Kc6 5 Bc3 g6 6 b4 Bb6 7 f3 Bc7 8 a4 Bb6 9 Bd4** The threat of exchanging into a winning pawn ending enables White to seize this useful diagonal. **9...Bc7 10 b5+ axb5+ 11 axb5+ Kb7** Or 11...Kd7 12 b6 Bg3 13 Kd5 Bf4 when 14 Be5 wins comfortably. Black's king should stop the pawn to strengthen resistance. **12 Kd5** The king has advanced, but now it has to cross a dark square to get to the kingside. The opposing bishop's grip on the diagonal must be challenged and a route opened up for the king. **12...Bb8** Rather than 12...Bf4? 13 Be5 Be3 14 Kd6 Kb6 15 Ke7 and the kingside pawns are ripe to be picked. **13 Bf2** Better than 13 Be5 Ba7 14 Kd6 when 14...Bb8+ stops the king march in its tracks. **13...Bc7 14 g3** Now that Black has no counterplay White can use his pawns to take away squares on the b8-h2 diagonal from the opposing bishop. **14...h5 15 h4 Bb8 16 b6!** Zugzwang! Black must now self-destruct, but even so White threatened to continue with f3-f4 followed by Bf2-d4-e5. **16...Kc8** If 16...f5 17 f4 then what can Black play? **17 Kc6 Be5 18 f4 Bb8 19 b7+ Kd8 20 Bb6+ Ke7 21 Bc7** and so on.

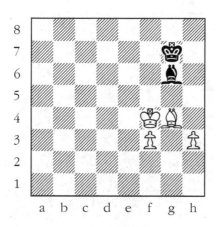

Diagram 6
Two pawns more, but...

This position arose in the game Fischer-Keres, Zurich 1959. Two extra pawns is naturally a big advantage but note that the h-pawn is the wrong rook's pawn so Black can aim to draw by giving up his bishop for the f-pawn and tucking his king in the corner.

Fischer points out that if it were Black to play he could draw with 1...Kf6 as White's king would be denied entry squares into the black camp.

1 Kg5 Bd3 2 f4 Be4 3 h4 3 f5? would allow an immediate draw with 3...Bxf5. **3...Bd3 4 h5 Be4 5 h6+ Kh8 6 Bf5 Bd5 7 Bg6 Be6** Keres tries to stop the f-pawn from advancing. **8 Bh5 Kh7 9 Bg4** Pushing the bishop away and earning the time to advance the f-pawn. **9...Bc4** After 9...Bxg4 10 Kxg4 Kxh6 11 Kf5 Kg7, advancing to the sixth rank with 12 Ke6 wins. **10 f5 Bf7 11 Bh5 Bc4 12 Bg6+ Kg8 13 f6 Bb3 14 Kf4 Bc4 15 Ke5 Bb3 16 Kd6 Bc4 17 Ke7 Bb3 18 Bf5** winning as 19 Be6 is coming.

In these two previous examples White's king was able to do useful work aiding the pawn or threatening invasion.

TIP: In bishop endings look out for potential king routes into the opposing camp, even if this may take many moves and thorough preparation.

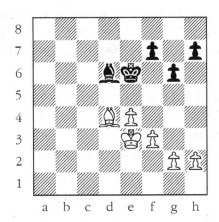

Diagram 7
With bishops; a draw!

Even with the 'right rook's pawn' White has no real winning chances. As Black I would be tempted to play ...h7-h5 but otherwise leave my pawns untouched on light squares until White advances and proposes pawn exchanges.

White cannot invade with his king and thus cannot attack the light squares in Black's camp.

TIP: In same-coloured bishop endings avoid placing your pawns on the same coloured squares as your bishop.

The Last Pawn

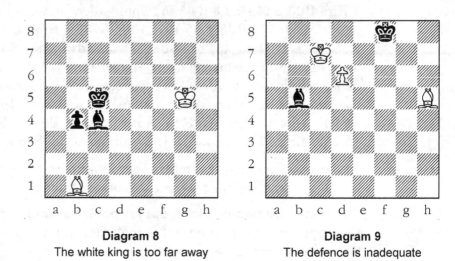

Diagram 8
The white king is too far away

Diagram 9
The defence is inadequate

In the ending of bishop and pawn against bishop, the position of the defending king is important. In San Segundo-Flear, San Sebastian 1995, it is just too far to intervene and stop the pawn edging through.

49...b3 50 Kf4 Kd4 Naturally holding up the white king's retreat and threatening ...Bd3. **51 Bg6 b2 52 Bb1 Bd3 53 Ba2** My opponent resigned as he has no defence to 53...Kc3 54 Ke3 (or 54 Kf3 Kc2 55 Ke3 Bh7 56 Ke2 Kc1 57 Ke1 Bg8) 54...Kc2 55 Kf2 Bc4.

White wins with the king on f8 (Diagram 9).

1 Bf3 Ba4 The pawn ending is lost following 1...Ke8 2 Bc6+ Bxc6 3 Kxc6 Kd8 4 d7. **2 Bc6 Bxc6 3 Kxc6 Ke8 4 Kc7** and the pawn queens. As Black was unable to get his king to d8 in the bishop ending, White squeezed away the bishop's defences with Bc6. However, Black can in fact stop this and hold such endings if his king is on c5 (instead of f8 in the initial position).

The next example illustrates a successful defence. Black resists his opponent's attempt to get his bishop to the d7-square. White can instead get his bishop to e8 but then Black defends by switching diagonals.

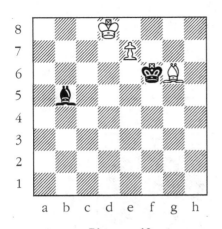

Diagram 10

Black draws by preventing Bd7.

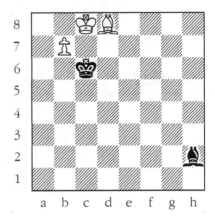

Diagram 11

Centurini's excellent study

In Diagram 10 White needs to play his bishop to d7, controlling the e8-square and enabling the pawn to advance. However, this proves to be impossible.

1 Bd3 Ba4 2 Bf1 Ke6! 3 Bh3+ Kd6 White now has another ploy. **4 Bg4 Bb5 5 Bh5 Ba4 6 Be8** But this fails to **6...Bd1 7 Bb5 Bh5** and so on. White never will be able to obtain full control of the e8-square.

TIP: With bishop and pawn against bishop, the best defence is to place the king *in front of* the pawn on an opposite-coloured square to the opposing bishop. Failing this Black can often hold by going *behind* the pawn and fighting to control the key square to stop the bishop's diagonal being shut-off.

With knight's pawns there are more winning chances because one of the two diagonals is very short (Diagram 11).

Black stops the pawn by controlling the long diagonal. If White were to cover the queening square by playing Bc7 he would win, but here getting the bishop to b8 wins too, as we shall see.

1 Bh4 Kb6 2 Bf2+ Ka6 Stopping the manoeuvre Ba7-b8. But Black's king is stretched between two important defensive tasks (covering a7 and c7) so a timely zugzwang breaks through. **3 Bc5!** Inviting Black's bishop out into the open. **3...Bg3 4 Be7 Kb6 5 Bd8+ Kc6** Just in time, but now White wins a crucial tempo. **6 Bh4! Bh2 7 Bf2** and White's access to a7 is assured. **7...Bf4 8 Ba7 Bg3 9 Bb8 Bf2 10 Bh2 Ba7** and now the problem of the very short diagonal a7-b8 comes to the fore. **11 Bg1** and White will queen.

More Advanced Ideas

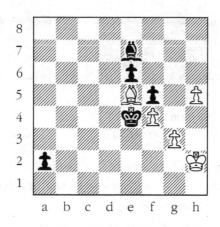

Diagram 12
The long diagonal is crucial

With rook's pawns the second defensive diagonal doesn't exist. In this recent example (Hakki-Flear, Tunis 1999) the a8-h8 diagonal counts for just about everything. White must defend a1 but at the same time he threatens to advance his h-pawn to h8, a square that he also controls.

48...Bd6 49 Ba1 Bf8 Black must first of all stop the h-pawn from advancing. **50 Kh3 Bh6 51 Kh4 Kd5!** 51...Kd3, heading for the white bishop, is promising but allows counterplay with 52 g4 Bxf4 53 g5. **52 Bf6 Kd6! 53 g4** Passive defence allows Black to carry out his primary idea: 53 Be5+ Ke7 54 Ba1 Kf7 55 Bb2 Bg7, when Black's control of a1 decides the game in his favour. **53...Bxf4 54 h6 Bxh6 55 g5 Bxg5+ 56 Kxg5 e5 0-1**

In Tukmakov-Timoschenko, USSR 1968 (Diagram 13), Black's f-pawn is a long way from its king. This factor gives White good chances to win.

1...Kg7 2 g5 hxg5 3 hxg5 A bishop cannot cut a king off on its own but with the help of a pawn it can sometimes construct an effective barrier. Here Black cannot get at the advanced g-

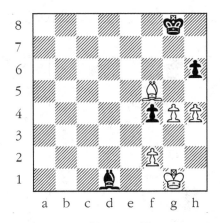

Diagram 13
White's plan is to capture the loose f-pawn

pawn. **3...Bh5** Coming round with the king doesn't help: 3...Kf7
4 Kg2 Ke7 5 f3 Kd6 6 Be4 Ba4 7 Kh3 Bd7+ 8 Kh4 Be8 (8...Ke5
9 Kh5) 9 Kg4 Ke5 10 g6 intending Kg5 and g6-g7 etc. **4 Kg2
Bg6 5 Bg4 Be4+ 6 Kh3 Kg6 7 Kh4 Bc6 8 Bd1 Bd7** Black
guards the g4-square. Instead of this, the pawn ending after
8...f3 9 Kg4 Bd7+ 10 Kf4 Bc6 11 Bxf3 Bxf3 12 Kxf3 wins for
White as 12...Kf5 13 Ke3! Kxg5 and 14 Ke4 does the trick. **9
Bc2+ Kg7 10 Be4 Be6 11 Kh5 Bd7 12 f3 Bh3 13 g6 Bd7 14
Kg5 Be6 15 Kxf4 Kf6** White has two extra pawns but some
care is needed as they are blockaded on light squares. If Black
plays passively then his opponent intends to advance his pawn
to f5 and then use his king to threaten to come to h6. **16 Kg3
Kg5** If Black just waits with 16...Bd7 then 17 f4 Be6 18 Kh4
Bd7 19 f5 Bc8 20 Kh5 Kg7 21 Kg5 etc. wins easily. **17 f4+ Kh5
18 f5 Bb3 19 f6 Kh6 20 Kf4** and White wins by coming to e7
with his king and advancing the f-pawn.

So despite the pawns all being on the same side, Black lost as
his f-pawn was so weak.

Try it Yourself

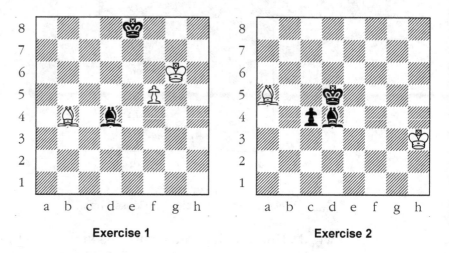

Exercise 1   Exercise 2

Exercise 1: After 1 Bd2 can Black draw?

Exercise 2: Can Black, to move, win?

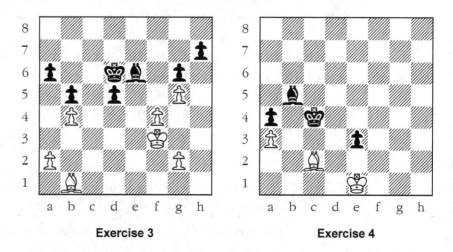

Exercise 3   Exercise 4

Exercise 3: White is to move. What is the likely result? Can you find a way to prove this?

Exercise 4: White to move is under pressure. Is he lost?

Summary

Pawns stuck on the same-coloured squares as a bishop, restrict the bishop, are exposed to attack and weaken the other colour-square complex.

The presence of the wrong rook's pawn for the attacking side helps the defence.

The fight for crucial diagonals often decides the struggle.

For an advantage to be decisive, the attacking king almost always needs to invade the opposing camp.

Chapter Six

Bishops of Opposite Colour

■ Converting Extra Material

■ Split Pawns

■ More Advanced Ideas

■ Try it Yourself

Opposite-coloured bishop positions, where one side has a bishop operating on light-coloured squares and the other a bishop covering the dark-coloured ones, have characteristics all of their own.

They are notorious for being very drawish, largely due to the fact that as half the squares on the board are hard to control, the win is often not possible with an extra pawn or more. Sometimes even if the king penetrates there is no way to release a blockade on the squares controlled by the opponent.

We shall see some examples of typical play where there are hidden chances to win. Winning ideas involve changing the pawn structure in such a way as to obtain a second passed pawn or tying the opponent down to create zugzwang.

In positions where there are two passed pawns it is still generally necessary to invade with the king to actively support one of the pawns. This is paramount as the bishop cannot support the passed pawn on squares controlled by the opposing bishop.

In endings each side has very little influence over the key squares patrolled by the opposing bishop, and this can lead to some surprising draws.

NOTE: Opposite-coloured bishop endgames are regarded as the most drawish of all types of ending.

Converting Extra Material

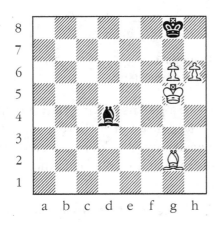

Diagram 1

Two extra pawns may not win!

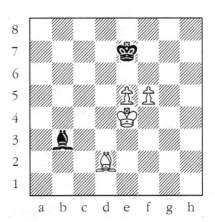

Diagram 2

A win as White's king can go either side

In Diagram 1 after **1 Bd5+ Kf8!** White cannot achieve anything. If h6-h7 at any point Black has a permanent blockade on the diagonal and if g6-g7+ then Black gives up his bishop for the two pawns. Nor can White hope to use his king to support the g6-g7 advance.

In Diagram 2 White's pawns are not as far advanced but he has the option of going either way with his king.

1 Bg5+ The bishop denies access for Black's king to the f6-square (in the case of a later e5-e6). Black's king now has to make a choice. **1...Kd7** If Black prefers the f-file then 1...Kf7 2 Kd4 Ba2 (2...Bc2 fails to 3 e6+ and 4 Ke5) 3 Kc5 Bb3 4 Kd6 Ba2 5 e6+ Ke8 6 f6 and wins. **2 Kf4** Heading the other way! **2...Ba2 3 Bh4 Bf7 4 Kg5 Ke7 5 Kh6+ Kd7 6 Kg7 Bd5 7 Kf6** Supporting the decisive advance e5-e6+.

White was able to win as he had two routes where he was threatening to penetrate with the king.

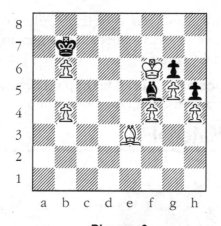

Diagram 3
Three useless pawns more!

Here White has *three* extra pawns, a king that has invaded and Black's pieces are both tied down. Yet there is no hope of winning this and similar positions. Black simply passes along the b1-f5 diagonal with his bishop and White cannot do anything on the key light squares.

NOTE: To hope to win White must normally have the potential to create two passed pawns.

Split Pawns

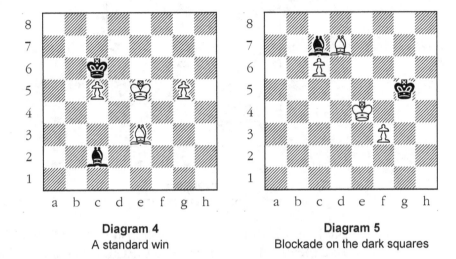

Diagram 4
A standard win

Diagram 5
Blockade on the dark squares

If the two passed pawns are widely separated and White can get his king through to support one of them to the queening square then White wins, as in Diagram 4.

1 Kf6 Bd3 2 g6 Bc2 3 Kf7 Bb3+ 4 Kf8 Ba2 5 g7 Bb3 6 g8Q Bxg8 7 Kxg8 Kd7 8 Kf7 Kc6 9 Ke6 Kb7 10 Kd7

In Diagram 5 Black can defend by stopping his opponent from advancing either pawn.

1 Kd5 Kf6 But not 1...Kf4? 2 Bg4 followed by Ke6-d7. **2 Bg4 Bh2 3 Kc5 Ke7 4 Kb5 Kd8 5 Ka6 Kc7** and Black keeps c7 and f4 well under control.

TIP: Black has better chances of saving the game if his bishop controls each pawn's advance.

With two isolated passed pawns, there are some points that should be borne in mind.

NOTE: Wrong rook's pawns increase the defensive possibilities; and the wider the passed pawns are spaced out the better the winning chances.

In Diagram 6 the pair of white pawns are not really dangerous as their threats are easily dealt with. However, the widely-spaced black passed pawns are too strong.

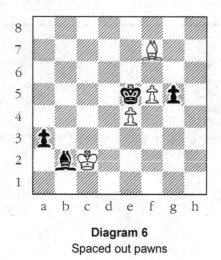

Diagram 6
Spaced out pawns

1 Kb3 Or 1 Kd3 Kf4 2 Ke2 Kg3! 3 Bd5 g4 4 Kf1 Kh2 5 e5 Bxe5 6 Ba2 g3 7 Bd5 g2+ 8 Bxg2 a2. **1...Kxe4 2 Be6** 2 f6 Ke5 and White's bishop stops his own pawn. **2...Ke5! 3 Bc8 Kf6! 4 Bd7 g4** and the f-pawn falls. Black will then win the white bishop for the g-pawn and he has the right rook's pawn.

More Advanced Ideas

Experienced players know that the loss of a pawn in the middlegame is often not too serious if they can reach an opposite-coloured bishop ending.

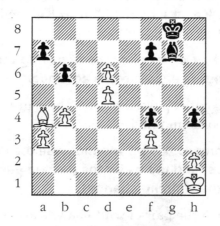

Diagram 7
An unusual pawn structure

TIP: When in trouble look out for ways to exchange pieces to reach opposite-coloured bishop endings even a pawn down.

This doesn't mean that all opposite-coloured bishop endings a pawn down are drawn!

My opponent had been forced to head for the ending in Diagram 7 in Flear-Etchegaray, Nice 1998, but felt that he could still draw. In order to win White has to establish a second passed pawn, either a passed h-pawn or something on the queenside.

35...Kf8 36 Bc2 Abandoning the forward d-pawn in order to maintain the queenside pawns. **36...Bb2 37 a4 Ba3 38 b5 Bxd6 39 Kg2 Bc5 40 Kh3 Bg1!** An interesting idea that is better than the passive defence of his own h-pawn. White eventually has to permit its exchange. **41 Kg2 Bc5 42 Kh3 Bg1 43 d6** Intending to keep Black's king restricted. **43...Ke8 44 Bf5 Kd8 45 Kxh4 Bxh2 46 Kg5 Bg1 47 Kf6!** 47 Kxf4? allows 47...Bh2+. Remember, it's not just the number that counts, it's the quality of the pawns! White's king is headed for the a7-pawn which Black has difficulty defending. **47...Bc5 48 Ke5 Bb4 49 Kd5 Ba3 50 Kc6 Bb4 51 Bg4 Ba3 52 Bh5 f6 53 Bg4 Bb4 54 Bf5 Ba3 55 d7 Bb4 56 Kb7 Bc5** The continuation 56...Ba5 57 Bg4 Bd2 58 Kxa7 Be3 59 Ka6 Kc7 60 a5 bxa5 61 b6+ Bxb6 62 d8Q+ Kxd8 63 Kxb6 a4 64 Kc5 a3 65 Bf5 Ke7 66 Kb4 Kd6 67 Kxa3 is equally hopeless for Black. **57 Be6 Bd4 58 Kxa7 Kc7 59 Ka6 Bc5 60 Bf5** Or 60 a5 as in the previous note. **60...Be7 61 a5 bxa5 62 b6+ Kb8 63 Kxa5 Kb7 64 Kb5 Bd8 65 Be4+ Kb8 66 Kc6 f5 67 Bxf5 Be7 68 Bd3 Bd8 69 Ba6 Ka8 70 Kd6 Bxb6 71 Ke7 Ka7 72 Bd3 Bc7 73 d8Q Bxd8+ 74 Kxd8 1-0**

TIP: Look out for plans that can lead to the creation of a second passed pawn. This is often the critical factor and can make the all the difference.

In Larsen-Hübner, Leningrad 1973 (Diagram 8), White has an extra pawn, but he only has one passed pawn. He has, however, a kingside majority which in the fullness of time may yield a second passed pawn. Black has his c-pawn which may cloud the issue, as may the fact that the a-pawn is the wrong rook's pawn.

This is a borderline case and it is hard to judge in advance what the outcome of the game should be. Let's see how play continued.

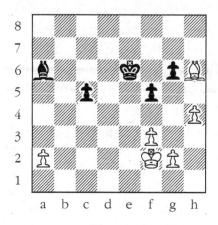

Diagram 8
What are the important factors?

1...Bb5 A passive defence that may be the wrong choice. Instead 1...Kd5 2 a4 c4 3 Ke3 c3 leaves White with no obvious way to make progress. **2 Ke3 Ke5** The annoying 2...Bf1 would oblige White to make an immediate decision about his g-pawn. **3 Bg7+ Ke6 4 Bf8 Kd5 5 Kf4** White heads for g5 in order to tie his opponent down to the weakness on g6. **5...c4** Following 5...Kd4 6 Kg5 Be8 7 Kf6 Ke3 8 Ke7 the bishop is forced away and after the further 8...Ba4 9 Kf7 the g-pawn falls. **6 Bg7 Ke6 7 Bc3 Bd7 8 Kg5 Kf7 9 a3** Zugzwang. If Black moves along the a4-e8 diagonal then White can play 10 h5 gxh5 11 Kxf5 creating a passed f-pawn. This seems to win as the black h5-pawn is then very weak. **9...Bc8 10 a4 Bd7 11 a5 Bc8 12 Bb2** Another zugzwang! **12...Ba6 13 h5 gxh5 14 Kxf5** Black resigned as the h-pawn falls immediately.

NOTE: In all endings, the choice between pursuing an 'active' or 'passive' defence is often critical.

In Ljubojevic-Karpov, Milan 1975 (Diagram 9), Black has an extra pawn but no real pressure, whereas White has no particular weaknesses. Therefore a draw would seem to be the logical result. In fact, it is hard to believe that Black can generate any serious winning chances at all.

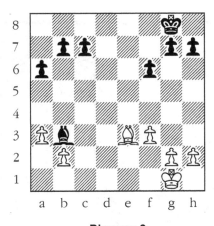

Diagram 9
What is happening here?

1...Kf7 2 Bf4 c6 3 Bd6 3 Kf2 Ke6 4 Ke3 Kd5 5 Bc7 looks to be a better defence, intending to meet 5...Kc4 with 6 Kd2. White's king should probably shadow the opposing monarch. **3...Ke6 4 Bf8 g6 5 Kf2 a5 6 Ke3 b6 7 h4 c5 8 g4?!** The kingside pawns should not be advanced too far as they can come under attack. Simpler is 8 Bh6 intending Bf4 and Bc7 just to harass the black queenside. **8...Bd1 9 Ke4 a4 10 h5?** 10 g5 looks better, putting the pawns on dark-squares. **10...gxh5 11 gxh5 f5+ 12 Ke3 Kd5 13 h6 Kc4 14 f4** Finally getting his pawns 'safe', but now Black's king causes dangerous threats. **14...Kb3 15 Bg7 Kc2 16 Be5 Bh5 17 Bf6 Bf7 18 Be5 Bb3 19 Bg7 b5 20 Bf8 c4 21 Bg7 b4!** A clever breakthrough that wins the bishop. **22 Kd4** No better is 22 axb4 c3 23 bxc3 (23 Bxc3 a3 24 bxa3 Kxc3 is a comfortable win as White's passed pawns are easily stopped) 23...Bc4! (blocking the long diagonal) 24 b5 a3 25 b6 a2! 26 b7 a1Q 27 b8Q (Black checks first and can force mate) 27...Qg1+ 28 Kf3 Bd5+ 29 Ke2 Qg2+ 30 Ke3 Qe4+ 31 Kf2 Qf3+ 32 Ke1 Qg3+ 33 Ke2 Bc4 mate! **22...c3 23 bxc3 bxa3 24 c4 a2 25 Kc5 Kb1 26 Kb4 a1Q 27 Bxa1 Kxa1 28 c5 Kb2 29 c6 a3 30 c7 Be6 31 Kc5 a2 32 Kd6 Bc8 0-1**

So, even if a position looks drawish a weakness in the pawn structure or an invading king may cause practical problems.

TIP: When defending, avoid unnecessary pawn moves as they may create weaknesses. When attacking look out for potential pawn breakthroughs that create dangerous passed pawns.

Try it Yourself

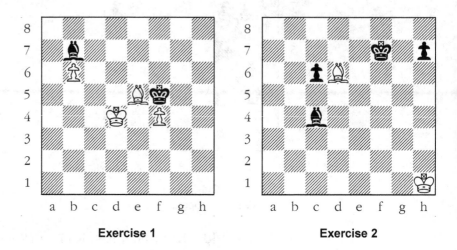

Exercise 1   Exercise 2

Exercise 1: White to move. What result?

Exercise 2: What result would you expect with Black to move?

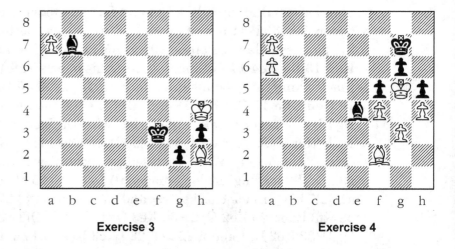

Exercise 3   Exercise 4

Exercise 3: Is there any point in Black continuing this position, or is it hopelessly drawn?

Exercise 4: Can White create a second passed pawn, and thus obtain excellent winning chances?

Summary

Opposite-coloured bishop endings are drawish.

To win, the attacking side must at some point obtain a passed pawn that cannot be permanently blockaded.

Usually two passed pawns plus an invading king will be necessary to undo the defensive blockade.

Chapter Seven

Bishop versus Knight

- **Bishops on Top**
- **Bishop and Pawn versus Knight**
- **Knights on Top**
- **Knight and Pawn versus Bishop**
- **Try it Yourself**

Bishops and knights are fundamentally different pieces. However, on average they have a similar value and the struggle between them can be complex. The relative strength of these pieces in a particular game will depend on positional factors, so let's mention some of these.

Factors that favour bishops include: wide-open diagonals, play on both wings and a split pawn structure. The most striking practical examples that favour knights are when the side with the bishop has to cope with its own pawns stuck on the same colour-complex as the bishop. Knights are excellent when the position is fairly closed, when the knight can secure a central foothold, or if play is on a limited front. They are much less effective when restricted to the edge of the board.

So much for the generalisations, let's see how these positional factors work in actual play.

Bishops on Top

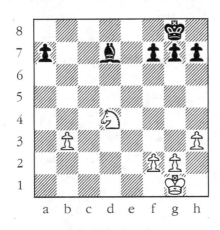

Diagram 1
The bishop is better

In an open position such as this (Stoltz-Kashdan, The Hague 1928), Black's bishop is the superior minor piece. However, with White having no weaknesses it isn't obvious how Black should try and win!

In fact with Black to move he is able to bring up his king for an active central role, and then by creating threats on both wings to put White under pressure.

1...Kf8 2 Kf1 Ke7 3 Ke2 Kd6 4 Kd3 Kd5 Black has the slightly more active king. White now decides to start moving his pawns off the exposed light squares. **5 h4 Bc8** Intending to come to ...a7-a6, whereupon White will have to decide which way to go with his king. **6 Nf3 Ba6+ 7 Kc3** If White goes the other way with 7 Ke3 then Black targets the b-pawn with 7...Kc5. **7...h6 8 Nd4 g6** Taking away useful squares from the knight. **9 Nc2 Ke4 10 Ne3 f5** The white kingside pawns are under pressure. **11 Kd2 f4 12 Ng4** After 12 Nc2 Bf1 13 Ne1 Black can still invade with his king: 13...Kf5 14 f3 g5 15 hxg5 Kxg5 followed by bringing the king to g3 to further attack the g-pawn. **12...h5 13 Nf6+ Kf5 14 Nd7 Bc8** Forcing the knight to make a difficult decision. **15 Nf8** Or 15 Nc5 Kg4 16 Nd3 Bf5 and Black wins a pawn. **15...g5 16 g3** 16 hxg5 Kxg5 is no improvement as Black's knight is stranded and, after the further...Kh6-g7, lost! **16...gxh4 17 gxh4 Kg4 18 Ng6 Bf5 19 Ne7 Be6** Black finally wins a pawn and so obtains a passed pawn that decides the game. **20 b4 Kxh4 21 Kd3 Kg4 22 Ke4 h4 23 Nc6 Bf5+ 24 Kd5 f3 25 b5 h3 26 Nxa7 h2 27 b6 h1Q 28 Nc6 Qb1 29 Kc5 Be4 0-1**

TIP: On an open board with possibilities on both wings, the bishop is the superior minor piece.

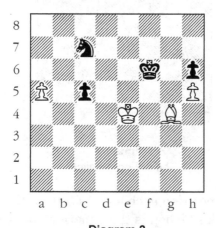

Diagram 2
The bishop is boss

White has only two rook's pawns (and by definition one of them must be the 'wrong' one, see Chapter Five!) but with threats on both wings and the better king Black is unable to cope (Liverpool-Glasgow, correspondence).

1 Be2 Ke6 2 Bc4+ 'Inviting' Black to choose which side he will go. **2...Kd6** 2...Kf6 3 Kf4 is zugzwang; if the knight moves the a-pawn advances unhindered, whereas if the king retreats White invades with his king. **3 Kf5 Nd5** Black aims to play actively with his knight. **4 Kg6 Ne3 5 Be2 c4 6 Kxh6 c3 7 Bd3** In order to give up the bishop, if necessary, for the c-pawn. **7...Ng4+** Or 7...c2 8 Bxc2 Nxc2 9 Kg6 Nd4 10 Kf6 Ne6 and the two rook's pawns beat the knight after 11 a6! **8 Kg5 Ne5 9 Bc2 Nc4 10 a6** and Black resigned.

If the position is blocked but the bishop can attack the opposing pawns then it is still the superior minor piece.

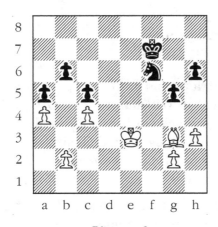

Diagram 3
Black's pawns are targets

In the game Konstantinopolovsky-Kasparian, Moscow 1942, White first attacks the base of Black's pawn chain with his bishop, thus tying down the knight.

1 Bc7 Nd7 Then White threatens invasion! **2 Ke4 Ke6** Now zugzwang is close, but Black must first be prevented from chasing away the king with 3...Nf6+. **3 Bd8 Ne5 4 b3 Nc6** Striving for some freedom. Instead 4...Nd7 5 g4 is zugzwang. **5 Bxb6 Kd6 6 g4 Nd4 7 Bxa5 Nxb3 8 Bc3** and White wins easily as Bg7 is threatened winning a second pawn.

In Diagram 4 White has a slight space advantage but cannot undertake anything very productive. There are no pawns to attack with the bishop and consequently White cannot tie down both pieces, so there is never a chance for zugzwang. If the white king goes to h6 Black defends on g8; if White heads for e4

Black comes to e6. So the position is drawn.

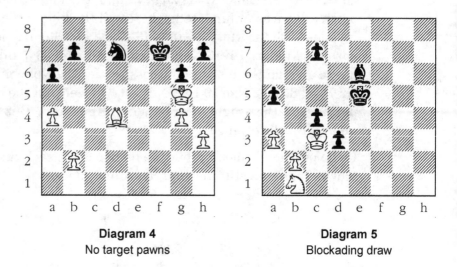

Diagram 4
No target pawns

Diagram 5
Blockading draw

With two extra pawns but nothing to attack, Black could not make progress in Wittmann-Flear, Graz 1984 (see Diagram 5). White shuttles backwards and forwards from d2. Note that the five squares b1, c4, e4, f3 and f1 cannot all be controlled by Black at the same time (wherever one places his king and bishop), so there is never any hope of zugzwang.

NOTE: On a limited front the knight is a good defensive piece, assuming it has room to manoeuvre.

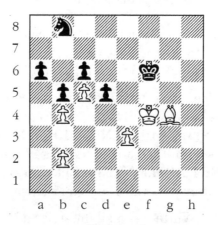

Diagram 6
Black is in zugzwang

In Flear-Birmingham, Paris 1989, Black's knight, dominated by the bishop, has no squares to manoeuvre and Black is immediately in zugzwang.

45 Bh3 Black resigned as 45...a5 46 bxa5 Na6 47 Bc8 Nxc5 48 a6 and 45...Ke7 46 Ke5 Nd7+ 47 Bxd7 Kxd7 48 Kf6 are both hopeless.

Bishop and Pawn versus Knight

In the ending of bishop and pawn against knight Black would naturally like to place his king on a blockading square that is the opposite colour to the opponent's bishop. If this is not feasible then attacking the pawn from behind is a good defensive try.

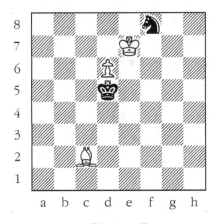

Diagram 7
Black scrapes a draw

Here in a study (Mandeleuilyu 1938), Black is denied 'nuisance' checks starting with ...Ng6+ and must be ready to meet the capture of his knight with the capture of the pawn.

1...Kc6! 1...Ke5 2 Be4! is already zugzwang, as is 1...Kc5 2 Be4. **2 Ba4+ Kc5 3 Be8 Kd5 4 Bf7+ Kc6!** Not 4...Ke5 5 Bh5 Kd5 6 Bf3+ Ke5 as White generates zugzwang with 7 Be4! **5 Bh5 Kc5** Black holds but he must get his timing right.

 WARNING: Be on the look out for zugzwang!

In Diagram 8 Black to play draws (Averbakh), not with 1...Nxd8? 2 c7 Nb7+ 3 Kd5 but with **1...Nd4 2 c7 Nb5+** and **3...Nxc7** Annoying checks and forks are useful weapons for the knight, but with White to move, there is always the possibility of zugzwang.

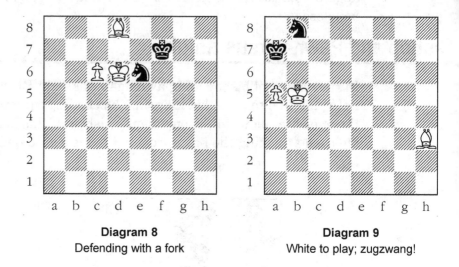

Diagram 8
Defending with a fork

Diagram 9
White to play; zugzwang!

1 Bb6 Stopping ...Nd4 for the moment. **1...Kf6 2 Be3 Kf7 3 Bf2** A passing move. **3...Kf6 4 Bg3!** The point is that Black is denied access to the d4-square. **4...Kf7** Not 4...Nd4? due to 5 Be5+. **5 Be5** and Black finds himself in zugzwang and loses quickly.

Diagram 9 (Averbakh) looks dead-drawn as Black's king is in front of the pawn on a dark square. However, after **1 Bc8** Black's knight is squeezed and lost! Note that White has the right rook's pawn and wins! A slightly contrived position perhaps (in the diagram, Black to play can avoid this tragedy in a number of ways) but a clear illustration that edges and corners can present real problems for a knight.

NOTE: The closer that a passed pawn is to the edge of the board, the greater the difficulty for a defending knight.

Knights on Top

I remember sitting next to this game (Lupu-Maes, Montpellier 1999 – Diagram 10) and being astonished that White could win.

Black's bishop is severely restricted by his pawns but he has only one weakness. Surprisingly, it's enough! **57 Nc4 Bf8 58 Ne3 Be7 59 Nf5 Bf8** In the game Black lost mundanely after

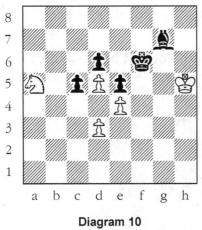

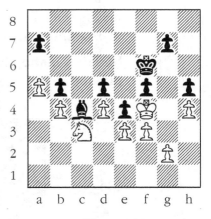

Diagram 10
The bad bishop

Diagram 11
Another bad bishop

59...Bd8 60 Nxd6 Ba5 61 Nc4 Bc3 62 Ne3 Bd4 63 Ng4+ Ke7 64 Kg6 Kd7 65 Kf6 Kd6 66 Kf5 c4 67 dxc4 Ba1 68 Nxe5. Maes resigned in view of 68...Bxe5 69 c5+ Kxc5 70 Kxe5. White now triangulates, as in a pawn ending. **60 Kh4! Kg6 61 Kg4 Kf6 62 Kh5** Black is thus pushed backwards. **62...Kf7 63 Kg5 Ke8** Or 63...Be7+ 64 Nxe7 Kxe7 65 Kg6 Ke8 66 Kf6 Kd7 67 Kf7 Kc7 68 Ke7 and the d-pawn falls. **64 Kf6 Kd7 65 Kf7** and wins.

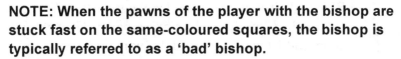

NOTE: When the pawns of the player with the bishop are stuck fast on the same-coloured squares, the bishop is typically referred to as a 'bad' bishop.

In Diagram 11 (Smyslov-Derkach, Kiev 1937) the pawns are on the same-coloured squares as the bishop. Furthermore, the black king is tied down to stopping the entry of its white counterpart. Zugzwang is near.

1 a6 Cutting out any ideas of ...a7-a6 defending the b5-point. **1...g6 2 fxe4 fxe4 3 g3** Zugzwang permits White to advance. **3...Ke6 4 Kg5 Kf7 5 Nd1** Bringing up the knight to deliver the knock-out blow. **5...Bf1 6 Nf2 Kg7** Or 6...Be2 7 Nh3 Bg4 8 Nf4 and wins. **7 g4 hxg4 8 Nxg4 Bh3 9 Nf6 Be6 10 Ne8+ Kf7 11 Nc7 Bd7 12 Nxd5 Bc6 13 Nc3 Kg7 14 Kf4** With a clear-enough win. Black has alternative defence in 2...dxe4 when the winning technique is somewhat different: 3 g3 Bd3 4 d5 Bc4 5 d6 (a decoy to open up access for his king) 5...Ke6 6 Kg5 Kxd6 7 Kxg6 Ke5 8 Kxh5 Kf6 9 Kh6 Bd3 10 Nd5+ Ke5 11 Kg7! A neat finish – the h-pawn advances in short order.

If the pawns are on the same-coloured squares as a bishop, this means that the pawns only help defend the same colour complex as the bishop.

NOTE: A bishop is bad, not just because it has limited scope, but due to the weaknesses on the other-coloured squares.

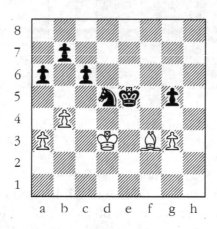

Diagram 12
An extra pawn in an open position

Black (Wojtkiewicz-Flear, Neuchatel 1998) has a well-entrenched knight and an extra pawn. However, the position is open and Black's queenside pawns may come under attack from the bishop.

47...Nf6 Hoping to attack White's g-pawn and force it to advance. **48 a4!?** Aiming to complicate. If 48 Ke3 then 48...Ne8 (with ideas of coming to c4 or f5) 49 Be2 Nd6 50 Bd3 Nb5 (the queenside pawns come under attack) 51 a4 (51 Bxb5 axb5 52 g4 b6 is a standard win) 51...Nc3 52 a5 Nd5+ picking up a pawn. **48...Nd5 49 Kc4 Nb6+ 50 Kb3 Kd4** The black king advances but White pins his hope on activating his bishop. **51 Bg4 Nc4 52 Bc8 Nd6 53 Bd7 c5! 54 a5** Rather desperate. The continuation following 54 bxc5 is instructive: 54...Kxc5 55 Be6 (after 55 a5 Nc4 56 Ka4 the blow 56...b5+! wins further material) 55...Ne4 56 g4 a5 (the white pawns are fixed on light squares and the knight and king easily outmanoeuvre their counterparts) 57 Bf5 Kd4 58 Bc8 Nc5+ 59 Ka3 b6 60 Bf5 Kc3 61 Bc8 Ne4 62 Bf5 Nd6 63 Be6 Nc4+ 64 Ka2 Kb4 65 Bd7 Ne5 winning a second pawn. **54...c4+ 55 Kc2 c3 56 Be6 Nb5 57 g4** 57 Bc8

can be met by 57...Kc4! with ideas of queening the pawn. Then if White defends with 58 Bxb7 Nd4+ 59 Kc1 c2 60 Kd2 Kb3 (threatening ...Kb2) 61 Be4 simplest is then 61...Kxb4.
57...Na3+ 58 Kc1 Nc4 59 Bc8 Upon 59 Kc2 Ne3+ 60 Kc1 Nd5 61 Bc8 Nxb4 62 Bxb7 Kd3 the queening of the c-pawn is assured. **59...Nd6 60 Be6 Kd3 61 Bd5 c2** White resigned as 62 Bb3 Kc3 63 Bxc2 Kxb4 followed by ...Ka5 is hopeless.

Knights can be particularly effective if the play is just on one wing.

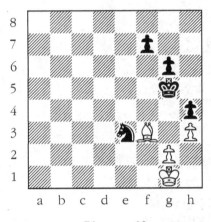

Diagram 13
To win Black must invade with his king

Despite the lack of pawns Black wins in such positions if his king can penetrate and attack the white pawns. Here (Liskov-Beilin, Moscow 1949) Black can force an entry.

1...Kf4 2 Kf2 Nf5 3 Bb7 Nd6 4 Bd5 Ne4+ Naturally the pawn ending is lost so White must move his king. **5 Kg1 f6 6 Bc6 Ke3 7 Be8 g5 8 Bd7 Ke2 9 Bc8 Ng3 10 Bd7 Ke1** A long tortuous route to get to the g-pawn but there is plenty of time. White can only wait. **11 Bc8 Ne2+ 12 Kh2 Kf2 13 Bd7 Nd4 14 Kh1** White can defend g2 but his king is very passive. Now Black, having maximised his piece disposition, can advance his pawns to increase the pressure. **14...f5 15 Be8 f4 16 Bd7 f3** By exchanging White's g-pawn, the remaining pawn on h3 is easier to attack and win. **17 gxf3 Nxf3 18 Bg4 Kg3 19 Bf5 Nd4 20 Bg4 Nc2 21 Kg1 Ne1 22 Be2 Ng2 23 Kh1 Nf4 24 Bg4 Nxh3** And the win is inevitable. For instance, 25 Bc8 Nf2+ 26 Kg1 h3 27 Bxh3 Nxh3+ 28 Kh1 Nf2+ 29 Kg1 g4 30 Kf1 Kf3 31 Kg1 g3

32 Kf1 g2+ 33 Kg1 Nh3+ 34 Kh2 g1Q+ 35 Kxh3 Qg3 mate.

 TIP: Knights are excellent pieces when all the play is on one side.

Knight and Pawn versus Bishop

With knight and pawn against bishop the bishop can some-times defend even without the king.

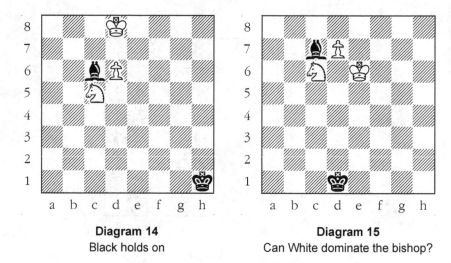

Diagram 14	Diagram 15
Black holds on	Can White dominate the bishop?

In Diagram 14 White cannot drive the bishop away in order to advance his pawn.

1 Kc7 Bb5 2 Nd3 Kh2 3 Ne5 With the threat of 4 Nc6. **3...Be8 4 Nd7 Kg3 5 Kd8 Bg6 6 Ke7 Bf5 7 Nc5** Threatening 8 Ne6. **7...Bc8 8 Nd7 Kf4 9 Kd8 Ba6 10 Kc7 Bb5 11 Nb8 Be8** and so on.

Black's king wasn't even needed.

In Diagram 15 the a5-d8 diagonal is shorter and the bishop can be driven off it, and thus the defence of d8 if the white king gets to b7. Black's king is, however, just close enough to prevent this plan, e.g. 1 Kd5 Kd2 2 Kc5 Kd3 3 Kb5 Ke4 4 Ka6 Kd5 5 Kb7 Kd6 and draws.

Averbakh however analyses a way to win starting with **1 Ke7! Kd2 2 Nd4 Ke3 3 Ne6** And the bishop is blocked out on either diagonal. **3...Bg3** Or 3...Ba5 4 Kd6 Bb4+ 5 Nc5 Ba5 6 Nb7 Bb6 7 Kc6 etc. **4 Ke8 Bh4 5 Nf8 Ke4 6 Ng6 Bf6 7 Ne7** Now the pawn will queen.

If the black king was closer to the pawn then there wouldn't be time for all this and Black would draw. In fact the proximity of the black king decides the result.

NOTE: With bishop and pawn against knight, the defending side will actively need the king to defend successfully. On the other hand, with knight and pawn against bishop, the defending king can be further away and a draw still obtainable.

It's not necessary to learn vast amounts of theory in these types of endings, just concentrate on the positive and negative qualities of the minor pieces. Even when a minor piece is superior it may still require a well-placed king to be able to convert any advantage.

TIP: When comparing the respective qualities of bishops and knights in your games, don't forget to consider the position and possibilities of the kings.

Try it Yourself

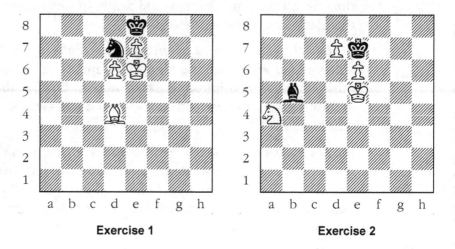

Exercise 1   Exercise 2

Exercise 1: Can White take away all of the knight's squares and thus win by zugzwang?

Exercise 2: Can White win? Remember Black threatens 1...Bxd7 as well as 1...Bxa4.

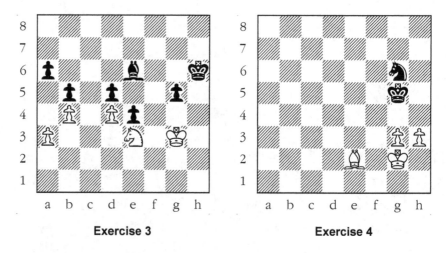

Exercise 3   Exercise 4

Exercise 3: Black to play. What result?

Exercise 4: Black to move. What result?

Summary

Bishops are stronger in open positions, especially if play is on both wings.

Blocked positions will favour knights if the bishop is restricted by its own pawns.

Knights are effective pieces if the play is only on one side of the board.

The bishop's long-range powers shouldn't be underestimated.

Knights can be restricted by the edge of the board or by a need to defend weak pawns.

The better minor piece generally needs a well-placed king to convert the advantage.

Rook Endgames

In most chess games the minor pieces join the fray earlier than rooks and are more likely to be exchanged in the early stages. This may explain why rook endings occur so frequently. Before we get down to looking at some examples, let's mention a few general principles:

☐ It's important to activate one's rook;

☐ A rook's place is behind a passed pawn, not in front;

☐ Rooks can harass or cut off the opposing king from afar;

☐ It's generally a good strategy to use the rook to create a barrier between the opposing king and passed pawns;

☐ A shelter for an attacking king is important;

☐ Rooks are particularly effective on the seventh rank (where they may attack pawns and cut off the opponent's king).

Rook and Pawn versus Rook

As we saw in Chapter Two, king and rook against king is a win, so in the ending of king, rook and pawn against king and rook, the typical winning plan is to win the rook for the pawn.

Firstly let's look at the ideal position for White.

Diagram 1
The Lucena position

This position was analysed many centuries ago. The black king has been prevented from approaching the passed pawn and White has been able to advance it to the seventh rank supported by his king.

Black's rook has taken up an active position behind the pawn and at present prevents White from venturing out of the shelter.

1 Rd2+ Ke7 1...Kc6 allows 2 Kc8 and the pawn queens. **2 Rd4!** Not a waiting move, White has something special in mind. Instead, if he ventures out into the open with 2 Kc7, then after 2...Rc1+ 3 Kb6 Rb1+ 4 Kc6 Rc1+ 5 Kd5 Rb1 White will have to go back again as otherwise the pawn falls. **2...Ra2** Black waits. **3 Kc7!** Only now is it time for the king to come out from the shelter. **3...Rc2+ 4 Kb6 Rb2+ 5 Kc6 Rc2+ 6 Kb5 Rb2+** Black harasses the white king for all he's worth, but now White inaugurates a new shelter for his king. **7 Rb4!** and Black is powerless to stop the pawn.

The Lucena position is a very useful one to know as it crops up frequently. The rook's manoeuvre is sometimes called 'building a bridge'.

Diagram 2
Playing for the Lucena position

White to play continues with 1 Kb6 followed by shuffling the pawn and king up the b-file until the Lucena position is reached.

Play is most interesting with Black to play, as he can try... **1...Ra8** ...when... **2 Kb6?!** ...gets nowhere after... **2...Rb8+ 3 Ka5 Ra8+.**

This illustrates a defensive ploy for a rook against a king and passed pawn: a series of harassing checks from the front, which is effective if there are at least three squares between the rook and pawn. White can win, however, even with Black to play, by meeting 1...Ra8 by **2 Rc4!** (defending the pawn) as 2...Rb8+ now fails to 3 Ka6 (or 3...Rc8 4 Rxc8 Kxc8 5 Kb6 Kb8 6 b5 etc.) 3...Ra8+ 4 Kb7 Ra1 5 b5 etc., leading to the Lucena position.

We can therefore see that if the defending king is prevented from getting in front of the passed pawn, then the defence has great difficulties. But what if the defending king has managed to take up a blockading position?

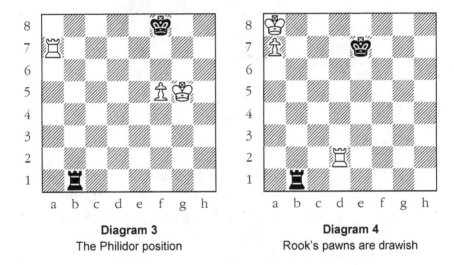

Diagram 3	Diagram 4
The Philidor position	Rook's pawns are drawish

Here Black's king is in front of the pawn but White's pieces are actively placed. Black has a clever drawing manoeuvre.

1...Rb6! Temporarily stopping the white king from getting to the sixth rank. Not instead 1...Rg1+ as Black then gets his king cut off from the pawn by 2 Kf6 Kg8 3 Ra8+. **2 f6** Threatening 3 Kg6. **2...Rb1! 3 Kg6 Rg1+** and White cannot win as he lacks a shelter from the onslaught of black checks.

Here we can see how pawns on the edge of the board are less useful. White's king can only exit the shelter via the b7- or b8-squares which Black controls. Black's king is even further away from the passed pawn than in the Lucena position but he can still draw.

1 Rh2 Kd7! 2 Rh8 Kc7 3 Rb8 Ra1 4 Rb7+ Kc8 5 Rb2 Rc1 and White's king cannot escape from the shelter (prison?) of the a8-square.

NOTE: Rook's pawns are more drawish in many rook endings, as the edge of the board limits the possibilities.

Diagram 5
Winning with a rook's pawn

White can win this one by taking control of the exit squares before Black's king comes across to spoil the plan.

1 Rc2 Ke7 2 Rc8 Kd6 3 Rb8 Ra1 4 Kb7 White escapes!
4...Rb1+ 5 Kc8 Rc1+ 6 Kd8 Rh1 But what's this, mate is threatened! Take note of White's following winning manoeuvre, which seems to baffle many of my students. **7 Rb6+ Kc5 8 Rc6+! Kb5** Capturing the rook allows promotion with check! **9 Rc8!** Defending the a8-square but also constructing another shelter. **9...Rh8+ 10 Kc7 Rh7+ 11 Kb8** The king is finally safe on b8 and the a-pawn is ready to advance. Black could have tried 2...Kd7, but White wins by fleeing in another direction: 3 Rb8 Ra1 4 Kb7 Rb1+ 5 Ka6 Ra1+ 6 Kb6 Rb1+ 7 Kc5 and after a few more spite checks White queens, i.e. 7...Rc1+ 8 Kd4 Rd1+ 9 Kc3 Rc1+ 10 Kd2 Ra1 11 a8Q.

More Pawns

Rook and four pawns against rook and three on the same side occurs frequently. White can create some pressure but with best play the game is drawn.

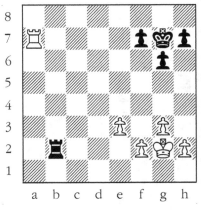

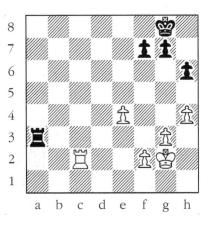

Diagram 6
Pawns on the same side

Diagram 7
White has practical winning chances

White will inevitably have to advance his pawns supported by his king. Black can best anticipate this with **1...h5!** when any pawn advances by White will lead to exchanges and limit his winning chances. A similar position with three pawns against two on the same side is even more drawish. Remember that if three pairs of pawns are exchanged we could easily obtain Philidor's position.

Here is an example of White managing to win this type of ending by making life very difficult for his opponent.

In Korchnoi-Antoshin, USSR Championship 1954 (Diagram 7), Korchnoi took the opportunity to gain space with **1 h5** Now Black has to be careful to earn the draw. **1...Ra5 2 g4 Ra7 3 Rc6 Ra3 4 f3 Ra5 5 Rc8+ Kh7 6 f4 Ra2+ 7 Kf3 Ra3+ 8 Kf2 Ra2+ 9 Ke3 Ra3+ 10 Kd4 Rg3?** Correct was 10...Rf3 11 Ke5 f6+ 12 Kf5 Rf1 and White cannot create a passed e-pawn. **11 Rf8 f6 12 e5 Rxg4 13 e6 Rxf4+ 14 Kd5 Rf5+ 15 Kd6 Rxh5 16 e7 Re5 17 e8Q Rxe8 18 Rxe8 Kg6 19 Kd5 Kf5 20 Re1** and White is winning as his king helps round up the pawns, e.g. 20...g5 21 Rf1+ Kg6 22 Ke6 g4 23 Rxf6+ Kg5 24 Ke5 h5 25 Rf8 g3 26 Rg8+ Kh4 27 Kf4 Kh3 28 Rxg3+ Kh4 29 Rg1 Kh3 30 Kf3 Kh2 31 Rg5 h4 32 Kg4 h3 33 Rh5 and Black loses his last pawn and the game.

TIP: The defence is not easy with four against three on the same side, but is more comfortable to defend if Black can avoid the big squeeze. So if possible play ...h7-h5.

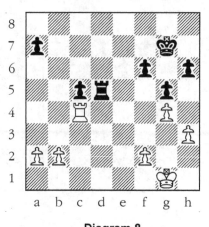

Diagram 8
The active rook

White has some pressure in Koch-Flear, Montpellier 1996, with a plan based around playing rook to a4 after first ferrying the king to the centre. Black could just sit there and wait and hope that White doesn't have anything more concrete or with... **28...Rd2!** ...he can sacrifice a pawn to activate his pieces! **29 Rxc5 Rxb2 30 Rc7+ Kg6 31 Rxa7 h5** White has an extra pawn but his opponent's active rook and well-organised kingside will be sufficient to draw. **32 gxh5+** After 32 a4 Ra2 33 Kg2 h4 34 Kf3 Ra3+ it will be too risky for White to run to the queenside and sacrifice the h-pawn. **32...Kxh5 33 Kg2 Rc2 34 a4 Ra2** The rook belongs *behind* the passed pawn. White's rook is tied down to the defence of the pawn and will eventually hinder the advance. **35 a5 Kg6 36 a6 Kf5 37 Ra8 Kf4 38 a7 f5** Black has carefully hidden his king so that the white rook on a8 cannot escape by giving check. White cannot hope to win so my opponent played... **39 Re8** ...and a draw was agreed.

TIP: In rook endings activating the rook at the cost of a pawn is often a better option than defending passively.

If it were White to play in Diagram 9 he would win with 1 Rf8+. Black to play can give a few checks but this only puts off the important question: Where should Black put his king?

1...Kg7! The king must go to the second rank, otherwise White will give check and then follow up with queening the pawn. If instead 1...Kf7 or 1...Ke7, White wins with a neat tactic 2 Rh8! Rxa7 3 Rh7+ skewering the rook.

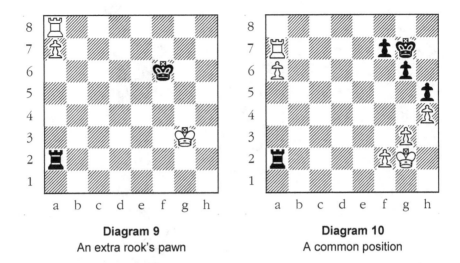

Diagram 9
An extra rook's pawn

Diagram 10
A common position

In fact in such positions the black king is only safe on g7 and h7.

White can try to walk his king to b6, to free his rook, but then after say Kb6 Rb1+, Kc6 Ra1 he cannot make progress. In the meantime the black king must stay on the two squares g7 and h7 and the black rook must keep the a-pawn in view from behind.

In Diagram 10 White has won a pawn and Black has prudently played his rook behind it. Although White has a shelter in front of the a-pawn and can switch the king across to support it, this will only be at the cost of losing part of his kingside. Black then has the possibility of obtaining a kingside passed pawn. Let's see a sample variation of how this might work.

1 Kf3 Kf6 2 Ke3 Ke6 3 Ra8 Kf5 4 Kd4 Rxf2 5 Kc5 Kg4 6 Kb6 Rb2+ 7 Ka7 Kxg3 Black's counterplay is then very dangerous and he is not worse. So the a-pawn seems to be too far away for this plan to work.

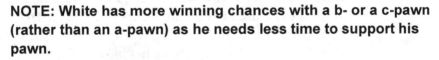

NOTE: White has more winning chances with a b- or a c-pawn (rather than an a-pawn) as he needs less time to support his pawn.

For an a-pawn to offer good winning chances, the white rook needs to get behind the passed pawn.

The ending Alekhine-Capablanca, Buenos Aires 1927, was particularly instructive.

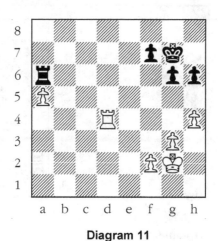

Diagram 11
Rook behind the passed pawn

1 Ra4 The rook is placed ideally behind the pawn. If Black's rook were to move away then the white pawn advances relentlessly. If White's king ever reaches b5 then Black's days would be numbered, so he uses his king to hold off the opposing monarch. **1...Kf6 2 Kf3 Ke5 3 Ke3 h5 4 Kd3 Kd5 5 Kc3 Kc5** Black has prevented a direct invasion on the queenside, but what should he do after... **6 Ra2!** Zugzwang! **6...Kb5** 6...Ra8 loses easily as pawn endings are hopeless: 7 a6 Kb6 8 a7 Rxa7 9 Rxa7 Kxa7 10 Kd4 Kb6 11 Ke5 Kc5 12 Kf6 etc. **7 Kd4** White switches to the kingside. **7...Rd6+ 8 Ke5 Re6+ 9 Kf4 Ka6** Black has succeeded in liberating his rook, but the white king is now threatening the kingside. **10 Kg5! Re5+ 11 Kh6 Rf5 12 f4** More precise was 12 Kg7 Rf3 13 Kg8 Rf6 14 f4 Rf5 15 Kg7 with zugzwang. **12...Rc5 13 Ra3 Rc7 14 Kg7 Rd7** Black holds on grimly. Alekhine now uses his f-pawn to break up the kingside and create a passed pawn. **15 f5 gxf5 16 Kh6 f4** A counter-sacrifice to hold the h-pawn. **17 gxf4 Rd5 18 Kg7 Rf5 19 Ra4 Kb5 20 Re4** Threatening 21 Re5+. **20...Ka6 21 Kh6 Rxa5 22 Re5 Ra1 23 Kxh5 Rg1 24 Rg5** Black's king is too far away for him to be able to defend successfully. **24...Rh1 25 Rf5 Kb6 26 Rxf7 Kc6 27 Re7** Cutting the king off on the e-file and allowing White to advance at his leisure. He will eventually obtain a version of Lucena's position.

TIP: The rook is generally best placed behind the passed pawn.

In the example we saw earlier in this chapter Antoshin was

unsuccessful in giving up his rook, even for three pawns, as Korchnoi was able to come back too quickly with his king. It is, however, a common theme that in a race one side has to sacrifice his rook for the opponent's dangerous passed pawn and the ending of rook against pawn(s) then follows.

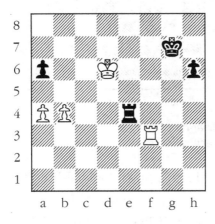

Diagram 12
Giving up the rook!

If the pawn is well advanced and supported by the king, a draw can often be earned, as in Van Mil-Flear, Oakham 1994.

49 Rb3! Behind the pawn that is ready to roll. **49...Kf6!** The king is headed up the board, not really towards the centre. **50 b5 axb5** 50...Rxa4 looks dangerous after 51 b6. **51 axb5 Re6+ 52 Kd7 Re7+ 53 Kd8 Rh7!** Getting ready to be sacrificed for the b-pawn. **54 b6 h5 55 b7 h4!** Gaining an important tempo on ...Rxb7. **56 b8Q Rh8+ 57 Kd7 Rxb8 58 Rxb8 Kf5 59 Kd6 h3 60 Rb4 Kg5 61 Ke5** and draws.

There are further examples of rook against pawn in Chapter Ten.

 TIP: Anticipate the rook sacrifice drawing idea by improving the king and advancing the pawn.

Rooks are powerful pieces and tactical tricks abound. Look out for mating nets, as in Diagram 13... **1...f4+ 2 Ke4?** 2 Ke2 is better but it's not yet obvious why. **2...Rd6! 3 Rxa7+** Or 3 Rxd6 Kxd6 4 Kf5 Kd5 and Black wins. **3...Ke6** Winning as mate with 4...Rd4 is threatened (Piskalnietis-Berzins, USSR 1962).

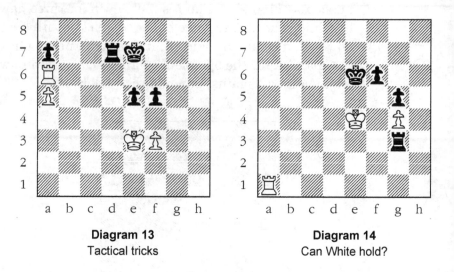

Diagram 13
Tactical tricks

Diagram 14
Can White hold?

In Diagram 14 the g-pawn looks difficult to defend, but there is a way!

1 Ra6+ Kf7 2 Ra4!! The alternative 2 Kf5 Rf3+ 3 Ke4 Rf4+ is hopeless. **2...Rxg4+** After 2...Kg6 then 3 Kd5 seems to hang on. **3 Kf5** and now... **3...Rxa4** ...is stalemate! Otherwise 3...Rg1 4 Ra7+ Kg8 5 Kxf6 g4 6 Kg5 is also drawn.

Converting an Advantage

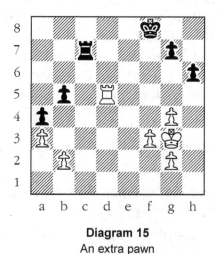

Diagram 15
An extra pawn

There now follows a few examples of the typical winning technique with an extra pawn or a positional advantage. In each case the player with the advantage tries to keep control of events and decide at which moment to exchange or simplify.

In Flear-Brook, Oakham 1988 (Diagram 15), White is a pawn up but, the win is complicated by the devalued g-pawns. It can be very difficult to make a passed pawn from a majority that includes a doubled pawn.

49...Rb7 50 Kf4 White first improves his king. **50...Ke7 51 Kf5 Rb6 52 Re5+ Kf7 53 Rc5 Rb7 54 Ke4** White keeps open his options of heading for c6 or advancing with f2-f4 and g4-g5 etc. Black is tired of waiting and decides to undertake active measures. **54...b4 55 Ra5 bxa3 56 bxa3 Rb2 57 g3 Re2+ 58 Kd3** After 58 Kf4 Black has counterplay with 58...g5+ 59 Kf5 Re3. **58...Rg2 59 Ke3** In order to tie down the black rook **59...Rxg3 60 Kf2 Rh3 61 Kg2 Rh4 62 Rxa4 h5** The only hope for freedom. **63 Rf4+ Kg8 64 a4 hxg4 65 fxg4 Rh6 66 a5 Ra6 67 Ra4** So the position clarifies. White has an extra passed pawn supported from behind. **67...Kf7 68 Kf3 Ke6 69 Ke4 g6 70 Kf4 Kf6 71 Ra1** Zugzwang forces concessions from Black. **71...Ke6 72 Kg5 Kf7 73 Kh6 Kg8 74 g5 Kf7 75 Kh7 Kf8 76 Rf1+ Ke7 77 Rf6** Exchanging the a-pawn for the g-pawn which leads to the Lucena position. **77...Rxa5 78 Kxg6 Rb5 79 Rf1 Rb2 80 Kg7 Rg2 81 g6 Rh2 82 Kg8 Rg2 83 g7 Rh2 84 Re1+ Kd7 85 Re4 Rh3 86 Kf7 Rf3+ 87 Kg6 Rg3+ 88 Kf6 1-0**

Practical endings often go through a series of phases in which the aims and advantages are changed and modified.

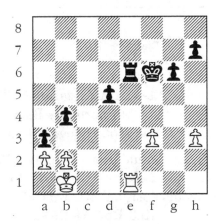

Diagram 16

Changing advantages

In Goldgewicht-Flear, Orange 1999, Black has won a pawn and has the better king but his isolated d- and a-pawns will require attention.

36 Rd1 Ke5 37 bxa3 bxa3 38 Rd3 Ra6 For the moment Black's rook must take up a passive role. **39 Kc2 d4 40 Kd2 h5 41 h4** Otherwise Black can play ...h5-h4, followed by ...Kf4 and ...Kg3 to create a passed h-pawn. **41...Kf4** Exchanging the d-pawn for White's f-pawn and thus freeing the king for a more active role. **42 Rxd4+ Kxf3 43 Ke1 Kg3 44 Re4 Kh3** Black now organises his pieces, aiming to exchange his a-pawn for Black's h-pawn. **45 Kf2 Rc6 46 Re3+ Kxh4 47 Rxa3 Rc2+ 48 Kg1 g5 49 Ra4+ g4 50 Ra5 g3 51 a4 Ra2 0-1**

Black wins easily with ...Kg4, ...h5-h4 and ...Kh3.

NOTE: Two connected passed pawns normally beat one passed pawn in rook endings.

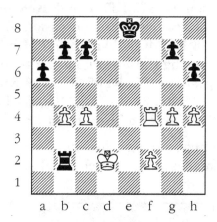

Diagram 17
The nagging edge

Here in Movsesian-Flear, Hastings 1996, White has a very slight space advantage, but normally Black's solid position would be expected to be good enough to draw.

42 Kc3 Rb1 Black should probably play ...Ra1 and ...a6-a5 to simplify things. **43 c5 Ke7 44 Kc4 Rd1 45 h5 Rd2 46 f3** White slowly improves his position. **46...Rd1 47 Rf5 Rd2 48 Re5+ Kf7 49 Re4 Rd1 50 Kc3 Rd5 51 Re1 Rd8 52 Ra1 Ke6 53 f4 Rf8 54 Re1+ Kd7 55 Re4 Ra8 56 Re5 Rf8 57 Re4 Ra8 58 Kb3** White is in no hurry. The longer the struggle the more likely Black is to make an error. **58...b6?!** Perhaps Black should just continue waiting with 58...Rf8, although White can play for f4-f5 and Re6-g6 with annoying pressure. Other tries are not good: 58...a5 59 b5 Re8 60 c6+ bxc6 61 bxc6+ Kd8 62 Rxe8+ Kxe8 63 Ka4 and 58...Re8 59 c6+ bxc6 60 Rxe8 Kxe8 61 Kc4 Ke7 62 Kc5 Kd7 63 g5 (zugzwang) are comfortable wins for White. **59 Re5 bxc5 60 Rd5+ Kc6 61 Rxc5+ Kb6 62 Re5 Rf8 63 f5 Rf7** Black has split pawns on the queenside and a passive position. **64 Kc4 c6 65 Re8 Rd7 66 Rb8+ Kc7 67 Rh8 Re7 68 Kd4 Rd7+ 69 Ke5 Re7+ 70 Kf4 Kd6 71 Rd8+ Kc7 72 Rf8 Kb6 73 f6** White's majority gets going whereas Black's is too slow off the blocks. **73...gxf6 74 Rxf6 Rh7 75 Kf5 Rh8 76 Rg6 Kb5 77 Kf6 Kxb4 78 Kg7 Rc8 79 Rxh6 a5 80 Rf6 a4 81 h6 a3 82 h7 a2 83 Rf1 c5 84 h8Q Rxh8 85 Kxh8 1-0**

I resigned as 85...Kc3 86 g5 Kb2 87 g6 c4 88 g7 a1Q 89 Rxa1 Kxa1 90 g8Q c3 91 Qg1+ Kb2 92 Qd4 wins easily.

A small advantage in rook endings can be enough if the opponent's rook is passive. Black missed an early chance to create play with ...Ra1 and ...a6-a5 and then was gradually outplayed.

TIP: In a passive position look for ways to exchange pawns to simplify the defensive task and look to get the rook active.

Diagram 18
Pawn structure problems

In Marshall-Chigorin, Barmen 1905, White has two isolated pawns and Black's pawn structure is compact and difficult to attack. **1...Ke6** A sensible move, centralising the king and increasing the pressure. Black could have snatched a pawn with 1...Rc3+ 2 Ke4 Rxa3 3 Kd5 but White's d-pawn supported by his king would give good counterplay. **2 Rb3 Kd5 3 Rd3 f5 4 h3 h5** White quickly finds himself in zugzwang. **5 Ke2 Rxd4** So Black wins the pawn after all but now under very favourable circumstances. **6 Rc3 Re4+ 7 Kd2 h4 8 Rc7 hxg3 9 Rxg7 Rxf4 10 Rxg3 Ke5 11 Ke2 Rc4 12 Rg6 Ra4 13 Rg3 f4 14 Rb3 Rc4 15 Kd1 Ke4 16 h4 f3 17 Ke1 Kf4 18 h5 Rc1+ 19 Kf2 Rc2+ 20 Ke1 Kg3 0-1**

The h-pawn can easily be handled with ...Rh2 and the f-pawn will soon queen.

WARNING: Don't grab a pawn 'just because it's there'. Instead weigh up the options: having an extra pawn in complications is often a less promising choice than maintaining and increasing a positional bind.

Try it Yourself

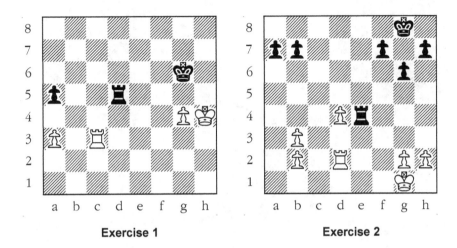

Exercise 1

Exercise 2

Exercise 1: Play continued 1...Rd6 2 Rc5 Ra6 3 a4. Could Black have done any better?

Exercise 2: White to play. Who is better and why?

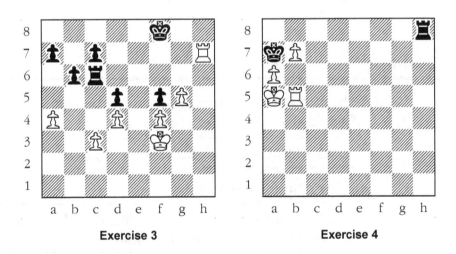

Exercise 3

Exercise 4

Exercise 3: A double-edged position in which White is to play, but who do you prefer and why?

Exercise 4: How does White win?

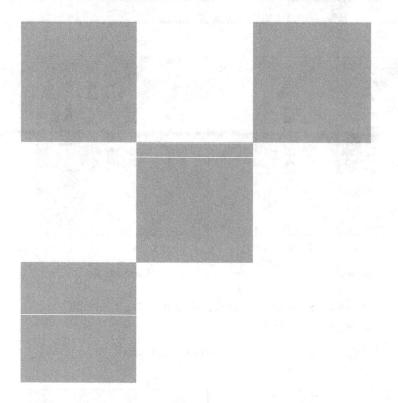

Summary

The attacking side often heads for the Lucena position, the defending side for Philidor's position.

A rook's ideal place is behind a passed pawn.

Activating the rook is important.

A rook is a long-range piece that can create barriers, attack pawns and harass the king from afar.

The attacking king will generally need access to a shelter.

If an extra pawn is a rook's pawn this is a drawish factor.

Chapter Nine

Queen Endgames

- Queen and Pawn versus Queen
- An Extra Pawn
- More Advanced Ideas
- Try it Yourself

In queen endings a passed pawn is a prized asset even if it is not yet very far advanced. The attacking queen can give active support and release blockades single-handed.

A centralised queen can dominate a position and make defensive checks difficult to sustain. Counterplay is usually a question of giving annoying checks or creating an opposing passed pawn. Because the queen is such a powerful piece, perpetual checks and mating themes crop up more than in other types of ending.

A common theme is the extended king walk: possibly to escape checks by seeking shelter in the far reaches of the board; or to attack a distant pawn; or even as a bold advance towards its counterpart to create a mating net.

Queen endings frequently arise as a result of a race in a pawn ending.

 TIP: In a pawn ending, which looks like it may transform to a queen ending, look out for the presence of passed pawns and open kings. If a king is exposed, ask yourself: Can it run away? Is there anywhere to run to?

Queen and Pawn versus Queen

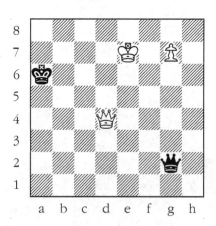

Diagram 1
The centralised queen

With queen and pawn against queen the main defence is perpetual check. The white queen is well placed in the centre and Black soon runs out of checks. The queening process doesn't take too long.

1...Qe2+ 2 Kd8 Qa2 3 Qf6+ Kb7 4 Ke7 Qa3+ 5 Kf7 Qa2+ 6 Qe6 Qf2+ 7 Ke8 and White cannot be prevented from queening.

White has more problems to find a shelter for his king if his queen is away from the centre.

With just queen and rook's pawn against queen there are excellent drawing chances as the pawn is not much help in shielding the king from a barrage of checks.

An Extra Pawn

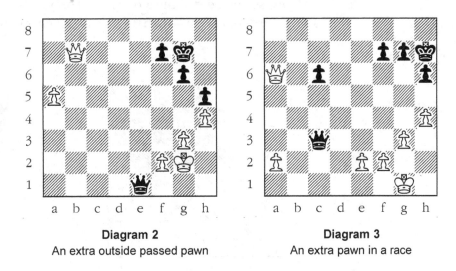

Diagram 2
An extra outside passed pawn

Diagram 3
An extra pawn in a race

Passed pawns can be actively supported by queens. Where one side has a passed pawn the only two possible defences are threats against the king or creation of a compensating passed pawn. In Diagram 2 Black can do neither and after **1 a6** his position is hopeless.

In Flear-Marciano, Toulouse 1996 (Diagram 3), White's extra pawn helps to safeguard his king and enables him to gain time due to the threat of 26 Qd3+.

NOTE: The presence of passed pawns for both players leads to a race where the key factor is the speed of the pawns as they advance towards their respective queening squares. Usually the most advanced pawn comes out on top.

Here it's a close one to call.

25...Qc1+ 26 Kg2 c5 27 a4 c4 28 a5 c3 29 Qd3+ g6 30 a6 c2 31 h5? Letting it slip. During the post-mortem, Hamdouchi pointed out an attractive win: 31 Qc4! Kg8 (31...Kg7 leads to mate by 32 Qc3+ Kh7 33 a7 Qd1 34 a8Q c1Q 35 Qah8) 32 h5! g5 (or 32...Qa3 33 hxg6 c1Q 34 Qxf7+ Kh8 35 Qh7 mate) 33 Qc8+ Kh7 34 a7 Qa1 and White wins by capturing on c2 with check! A clever exploitation of Black's slightly more exposed king. **31...Qd1 32 hxg6+ fxg6 33 a7 c1Q** and a draw was agreed as 34 Qxd1 Qxd1 35 a8Q Qxe2 leaves the position completely equal.

In queen endings a blockade of a passed pawn is only a temporary solution, so the best chance of counterplay is to push one's own pawn or create threats such as perpetual check against the opposing king.

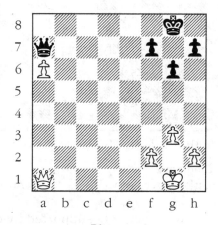

Diagram 4
White releases the blockade

White has the winning threat of Qa1-a5-b5-b7, forcing the black queen to flee, and then to continue by pushing the a-pawn home.

More Advanced Ideas

In Flear-Renet, Clichy 1993 (Diagram 5), White has a very exposed king. His main asset is an advanced pawn which will be even stronger in a pure queen ending.

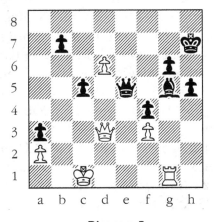

Diagram 5
The power of the passed pawn

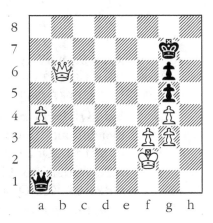

Diagram 6
Where to shelter the king?

34 Rxg5! Qxg5 35 Qe4! Threatening the exchange of queens on e7. **35...Kh6?** Black should take the draw with 35...Qg1+ 36 Kd2 Qf2+ 37 Kd1 Qf1+. **36 d7 Qf6?** Black should have tried 36...Qg1+ or 36...h4. **37 Qd5 Qb2+ 38 Kd1 Qb1+ 39 Ke2 Qc2+ 40 Qd2 Qc4+ 41 Kf2 1-0**

White, three pawns down, even managed to win with a very open king. Black had two protected passed pawns but they never moved!

My opponent, who was in time-trouble, rather optimistically wanted to win, but he had underestimated the importance of White's d-pawn.

TIP: It is the most advanced passed pawn, not the number of pawns, which promises the initiative in queen endings.

In Diagram 6 White has two extra pawns but his king is lacking a reliable shelter (Alekhine-Euwe, Nottingham 1936). If White tries to simply support and advance the a-pawn then his king will come in for too many checks. White finds a plan involving four mini-plans:

1. Advance the kingside pawns;

2. Use the queen to defend both wings;

3. Advance the a-pawn when possible;

4. March forward with the king to create threats and find shelter in the black camp.

1 Qb4 Qh1 2 Qe1 Qh2+ 3 Ke3 Kh7 4 a5 Qa2 5 Qd2 Qa1 6 Ke2 Kh6 7 f4 gxf4 8 gxf4 Qa4 9 Kf2 White delays the advance to g5 to ensure that Black cannot go forward with his king. 9...Kh7 10 g5 Qa3 11 Qd7+ Kh8 12 Qc8+ Kh7 13 Qc7+ Kh8 14 Ke2 Qa2+ 14...Kg8, awaiting events, is well met by 15 Kd2 Kf8 16 Qd8+ Kg7 17 Qf6+ Kh7 18 a6. 15 Ke3 Qb3+ 16 Kd4 Qb4+ 17 Kd5 Qb5+ 18 Kd4 Qa6 If 18...Qb4+ White avoids repetition with 19 Ke5 Qb5+ 20 Kd6 Qd3+ 21 Ke7 and now if 21...Qe4+ then 22 Qe5+. 19 Qb6 Qc8 20 Qd6 20 Qxg6? risks stalemate if Black sacrifices his queen! 20...Qc2 21 a6 Qd2+ 22 Ke5 Qc3+ 23 Ke6 Qc8+ 24 Ke7 Kh7 25 Qd7 and if now 25...Qxa6 then 26 Kf8+ Kh8 27 Qg7 mate.

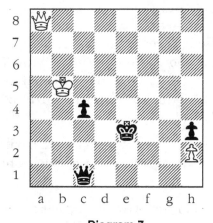

Diagram 7
Give me shelter

Diagram 8
The changing role of the king

In Diagram 7 (Rouchouse-Flear, Montpellier 1997), Black must advance the c-pawn and seek a plausible shelter for his king.

52...c3 53 Qe8+ Kf2 54 Qg6 Qf4! Covering some vital squares around his own king. **55 Ka5 Ke2 56 Qc2+ Qd2 57 Qe4+ Kf2 58 Qh4+ Kg1!** Capturing h-pawns isn't important, escaping checks is. **59 Qg3+ Kh1** White resigned as after 60 Qf3+ (60 Qxh3 c2+ is check!) 60...Kxh2 Black can escape the checks.

In Diagram 8 (Hauchard-Lepelletier, Narbonne 1997), the b-pawn is Black's weak point. However, in order to win the pawn White will need to attack it with his king!

First of all, to prepare the king walk White organises the defence of his kingside with the queen.

55...Qd3+ 56 Kg4 Qe2+ 57 f3 Qf2 58 Qc8+ Kh7 59 Qf5+ Kh8 60 Qd5 Kh7 61 h5 Kh8 62 Kf4 Qg1 63 Qa8+ Kh7 64 Qe4+ Kh8 65 Qe3 Qf1 66 Qe8+ After 66 Qxb6?! Qc4+ White will have to shed a pawn or two to get his king to safety. **66...Kh7 67 Qc6 Qg1 68 g4** Now Hauchard has finished the preparation for the king's adventure. **68...Qh2+ 69 Kf5 Qe2 70 Kf4 Qh2+ 71 Ke4 Qe2+ 72 Kd4 Qd2+ 73 Ke5 Qd8 74 Ke6 Kh8 75 Kf7 Qg8+ 76 Ke7 Qa2 77 Kd8** More precise than 77 Qxb6?! Qe2+, as White doesn't need to give his opponent anything. **77...Qa7 78 Kc8 Kh7 79 Qb7 Qa5 80 Qe4+ Kh8 81 Qe8+ Kh7 82 Kb7 Qd2 83 Qe4+ Kh8 84 Kxb6** The pawn finally falls. Now White's task is to gradually advance the pawn and avoid perpetual check. **84...Qd8+ 85 Kb7 Qd7+ 86 Ka6 Qc8+ 87 Qb7 Qf8 88 Qc6 Qa3+ 89 Kb7 Qe7+ 90 Qc7 Qe3 91 Qc8+ Kh7 92 Qf5+ Kh8 93 Qe4 Qd2 94 b6 Qa5 95 Qe6 Qa3 96 Kb8 Kh7** 96...Qxf3 allows 97 Qc8+ Kh7 98 Qf5+ exchanging queens. **97 Qe4+ Kh8 98 Qc6 Kh7 99 Qe4+ Kh8 100 b7** Look where White now finds shelter from the checks! **100...Qd6+ 101 Kc8 Qf8+ 102 Kd7 Qf7+ 103 Kc6 Qf6+ 104 Kd5 Qf7+ 105 Kd4 Qf6+ 106 Ke3 Qc3+ 107 Kf2 Qc5+ 108 Kg2 1-0**

The checks are finished and the pawn will soon queen. White's use of his king was instructive.

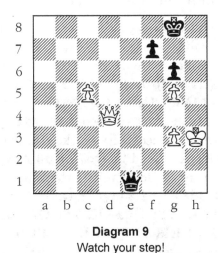

Diagram 9
Watch your step!

The continuation of Borisenko-Simagin, Moscow 1955, was as follows:

1...Qf1+ 2 Kg4? Trying to wriggle out of the checks, but falling for something horrible. However, after 2 Kh2 Qe2+ with the king so open and the black queen so active White probably can't win. **2...f5+! 3 gxf6 Qf5+ 4 Kh4 Qh5 mate**. A tragedy for Borisenko. A queen, when given a little help, can deliver mate, so be careful where you wander with your king!

WARNING: King walks can be dangerous for your health.

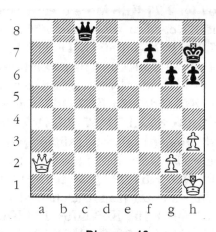

Diagram 10
Pawns on the same wing

With best play this position (Ciocaltea-Unzicker, Moscow 1956) should be a draw, but Black risks nothing in trying to win.

1...Qc1+ 2 Kh2 Qf4+ 3 g3 Simpler was 3 Kh1 to keep the structure as solid as possible. **3...Qf3 4 h4 h5 5 Qd2 Kg7** Black hopes to go walkabout with his king and create attacking chances. **6 Qd4+ Qf6 7 Qd2 Qe5 8 Kg2 Kf6 9 Qd8+ Kf5 10 Qd7+ Qe6 11 Qb5+ Qe5 12 Qd7+ Qe6 13 Qb5+ Kf6 14 Qg5+ Kg7** If at first you don't succeed... **15 Qd2 Qc4 16 Kh2** 16 Qd8! stops any king advance in its tracks. **16...Kf6 17 Qd8+ Ke6 18 Qe8+ Kf5 19 Qd7+ Ke4 20 Qe7+ Kd3 21 Qa3+ Kc2 22 Qe7** Much better was 22 Qd6! cutting the king off from the kingside. **22...Kd1 23 Qd8+ Ke2 24 Qe7+ Qe6 25 Qb7 Kf2 26 Qg2+ Ke1 27 Qg1+ Ke2 28 Qg2+ Kd3 29 Qf3+ Kd2 30 Qf4+ Ke2 31 Qc7 f5 32 Qc2+ Kf3 33 Qg2+ Ke3 34 Qb2 Qc4 35 Qa3+ Qd3 36 Qc5+ Kf3 37 Qc6+ Qe4 38 Qc3+ Kf2 39 Qc5+ Qe3 40 Qc2+ Qe2 41 Qc6 Kf1+ 42 Kh3 Kg1 43 Qc5+ Qf2 44 Qe3** A last gasp stalemate try which fails to **44...f4!** White resigned.

Positional advantages are relevant if the opponent is denied any tactical counter-chances.

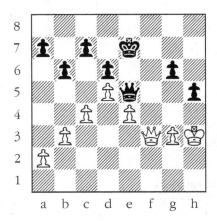

Diagram 11
A positional advantage for Black

In Keres-Alekhine, Dresden 1936, Black has a mobile 2-1 pawn majority whereas White's 5-4 queenside is nigh on impossible to get moving with the black queen so well installed.

1 Qf4 Qf6 The pawn ending after 1...Qxf4 2 gxf4 gives Black no winning chances. **2 Qh6 Kf7 3 Kg2** After 3 Qh7+ Qg7 the pawn ending will this time be winning as Black's king will eventually invade. **3...Qb2+ 4 Kh3 Qa1!** Forcing White's queen to come back and defend. **5 Qf4+ Kg7 6 Qf3 Qf6** 6...Qxa2? loses the initiative to 7 Qc3+ Kf7 8 e5. **7 Qe2 Kh6 8 Kg2 g5** Finally the pawns get moving. **9 b4 Qe5 10 Qf3 Kg6 11 g4?!** 11 a3, just consolidating and waiting, was a better try. **11...hxg4 12 Qxg4 Qb2+ 13 Kf3 Qa3+ 14 Ke2 Qxa2+ 15 Kd3 Qb3+ 16 Kd4 Qb2+ 17 Kd3 Qf6** Black has an extra pawn but there are some technical difficulties as his c-pawn is weak and his king rather open to annoying checks. **18 b5 Qf4 19 Qe6+ Kh5 20 Qh3+ Qh4 21 Qf3+ Qg4 22 Qf7+ Kh4 23 Qxc7 Qf3+ 24 Kd4 Qf6+ 25 Kd3 g4 26 Qh7+ Kg5 27 Qg8+ Kf4 28 Qe6 Kg5 29 e5!?** 29 Qg8+ Qg6 30 Qd8+ Kf4 31 Qf8+ Kg3 32 Qf1 may be a better chance. **29...Qxe5 30 Qxe5+ dxe5 31 Ke4 Kf6 32 Ke3 Kf5 33 Kf2 e4 34 Ke2 g3 35 Ke3 Kg4 36 d6 g2 37 Kf2 Kh3 38 d7 e3+ 39 Kf3 g1Q 40 d8Q** Another queen ending! **40...Qf2+ 41 Ke4 e2 42 Qd7+ Kg2 43 Qg4+ Kf1** and wins.

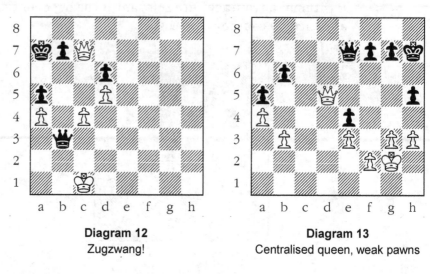

Diagram 12
Zugzwang!

Diagram 13
Centralised queen, weak pawns

In Diagram 12 (Flear-Gofshtein, Montpellier 1998), my opponent surprised me with **44...Qb4!** whereupon I had no good moves. Black thus wins a pawn without allowing any counterplay. Instead 44...Qxa4 45 Qxd6 Qxc4+ 46 Kb2 a4 47 Qe5 is still better for Black but less clear. **45 Qc8 Qxa4 46 Qg4 Qb4 47 Qd4+ Ka6 48 Qd3 Qc5 49 Kd2 a4 50 Kd1 Ka5 51 Qc3+ Qb4 52 Qd4 b6** The a-pawn will advance and there was no reason to play on, so I resigned.

In Diagram 13 (Levenfish-Alatortsev, Moscow 1947), White's well-placed queen bears down on e4, f7 and h5. This in itself is insufficient to win as Black can probably hold by stopping the white king from increasing the pressure.

1...g6 2 g4 hxg4 3 hxg4 f6? Better was 3...g5! as White's king cannot then hope to invade via f4. If then 4 f3 (what else?) 4...exf3+ 5 Kxf3 doesn't really look like an advantage for White. **4 Qc6 Qb4 5 Qxf6 Qxb3 6 Qe7+ Kh6 7 Qxe4** White wins a pawn but Black is staking all on creating a passed pawn. **7...b5 8 Qf4+ Kh7 9 Qc7+ Kh6 10 Kg3!** With mate threats in the air. **10...Qb4** 10...Qxa4 fails to 11 g5+ Kxg5 (11...Kh5 loses after 12 f4!) 12 Qe5+ Kh6 13 Qh8+ Kg5 14 f4+ etc. **11 Qe5!** Now 11 g5+ Kh5 12 f4 only draws after 12...Qe1+. **11...Kh7 12 Qxb5 Qxb5 13 axb5 a4 14 b6 a3 15 b7 a2 16 b8Q a1Q 17 Qc7+ Kh6 18 Qf4+ g5 19 Qd4 Qg1+ 20 Kf3 Qh1+ 21 Ke2 Qc6 22 Qh8+ Kg6 23 Qh5+ Kf6 24 Qh6+ Ke5 25 f4+!** Foiling the stalemate trick and winning.

Try it Yourself

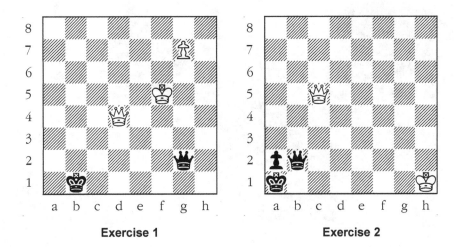

Exercise 1   **Exercise 2**

Exercise 1: On general considerations, should White win? After **1...Qf1+** do you have any ideas as to how play might go?

Exercise 2: What's the likely result after **1...Qd2**? Use your knowledge and feelings, plus some analysis(!) to justify your assessment.

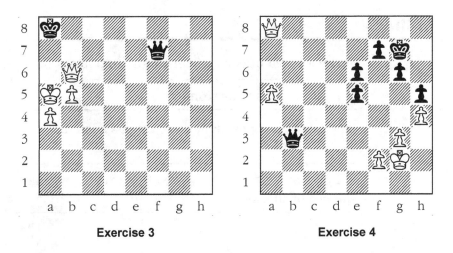

Exercise 3   **Exercise 4**

Exercise 3: Has Black to move any hope of saving the game?

Exercise 4: White to move. What result and why?

Summary

A centralised queen controls many important squares.

A passed pawn is a strong asset.

The queen is a powerful piece and as such mates and stalemates abound.

If kings are exposed they are often greeted with a long sequence of checks.

Chapter Ten

Pieces versus Pawns

The majority of games in which one side has an extra piece are fairly one-sided affairs. However, in positions with very few pawns or with the presence of a compensating dangerous passed pawn, the result can be less clear. Sometimes a strong passed pawn can save the day and even on occasion win the game, since badly placed pieces may not be able to get untangled or to rush back in time. Stalemate is another important theme in this chapter.

The endings in this chapter are typically the result of simplification from positions that can occur in other chapters. Naturally, before we head off down a forcing line it's wise to judge if this simplification leads to the desired result or not. So knowledge of the themes and techniques highlighted here will complement ideas developed earlier. A couple of noteworthy draws that we have already come across should whet the appetite for a chapter of surprises!

Knights and Pawns

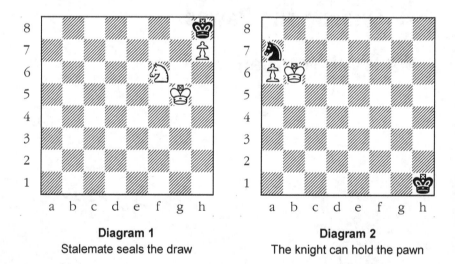

Diagram 1
Stalemate seals the draw

Diagram 2
The knight can hold the pawn

In Diagram 1 stalemate results if White's king approaches. Most endings with an extra piece and a pawn are wins, but this a significant special case. On the sixth rank, a rook's pawn can be stopped by a blockading knight, without the help of its king (Diagram 2).

1...Nc8+ 2 Kb7 Nd6+ 3 Kc6 Nc8 4 Kc7 Na7 5 Kb7 Nb5 6 Kb6 Nd6 7 a7 Nc8+ and draws.

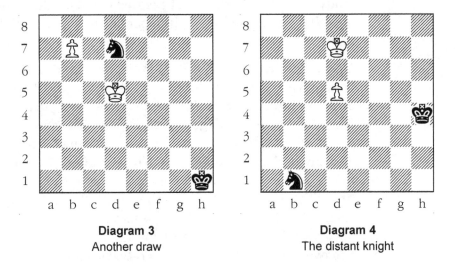

Diagram 3
Another draw

Diagram 4
The distant knight

Against non-rook's pawns (Diagram 3), the defending knight can even stop a pawn on the seventh from advancing. **1 Kd6 Nb8 2 Kc7 Na6+ 3 Kb6 Nb8** and so on.

If the knight is far away it may struggle to get back. In Diagram 4 the black king is poorly placed and this allows White to queen with check. **1 d6 Nc3** Or 1...Nd2 2 Kc7 Ne4 3 d7 Nc5 4 d8Q+. This line suggests that if the black king were on h3 (instead of the unfortunate h4) he would now draw by forking. **2 Kc6!** Placing the king to hold off the knight's retreat and at the same time avoiding checks. **2...Ne2 3 d7 Nd4+ 4 Kd5** and wins.

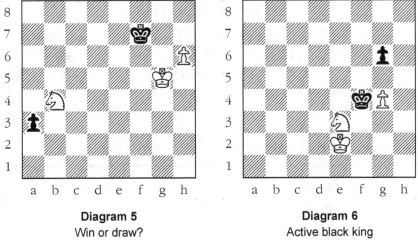

Diagram 5
Win or draw?

Diagram 6
Active black king

With knight and pawn against lone pawn there are drawing chances if either knight or king are distant. In Grigoriev's study (Diagram 5) the knight is tied down on the other wing but White can sometimes (it depends on zugzwang!) deliver mate.

1 Na2 Passing. **1...Kf8 2 Kf6!** Well calculated as 2 Kg6? Kg8 3 Nb4 (3 h7+ Kh8 4 Nb4 a2 5 Nxa2 is stalemate) 3...Kh8 4 Nc6 a2 5 Ne5 a1Q 6 Nf7+ Kg8 7 h7+ Kf8 8 h8Q+ only draws after 8...Qxh8 9 Nxh8. **2...Kg8 3 Kg6 Kh8 4 Nb4** Now 4...a2 loses easily after 5 Nxa2 followed by coming over to help out the king and pawn. So... **4...Kg8 5 h7+ Kh8 6 Nc6 a2 7 Ne5 a1Q 8 Nf7 mate.** It was all a question of timing, as in the original position, if it were Black to move then 1...Kg8 2 Kg6 Kh8 draws easily. The knight cannot 'lose a move' and it was only the manoeuvre 2 Kf6 followed by 3 Kg6 that enabled White to time his hop over to the mating square f7. So we can conclude that 1 Na2 is an accurate move that produces an immediate zugzwang.

In Diagram 6 White has difficulties to convert the advantage, as his knight defends the pawn but in turn requires defence by the king.

How can he win? White to play engineers a winning pawn ending.

1 Kf2 g5 Or 1...Ke4 2 Ng2 Ke5 3 Ke3 and Black is driven back and will soon lose his pawn. **2 Ke2 Ke4 3 Kd2 Kf4** Instead after 3...Kd4 4 Nf5+ Ke4 5 Kc3 Kf4 then 6 Nh6 wins comfortably. **4 Kd3 Kf3 5 Kd4 Kf4 6 Kd5! Kxe3 7 Ke5 Kf3 8 Kf5** and wins. The knight played the role of a decoy.

White doesn't always win such positions. In fact, in the diagram, Black to move has a study-like draw with 1...Kg3! and White cannot win: 2 Kd3 Kf3 3 Kd4 Kf4 and 4 Kd5 doesn't work.

Bishops and Pawns

With pawn against bishop, there is usually no problem to stop the pawn. In Diagram 7 (a study by Horwitz & Kling) Black has to be on his guard hold the game after... **1 Ka6** ...with... **1...Be4! 2 b7** Or 2 Ka7 Kd7. **2...Kc7** and the pawn falls.

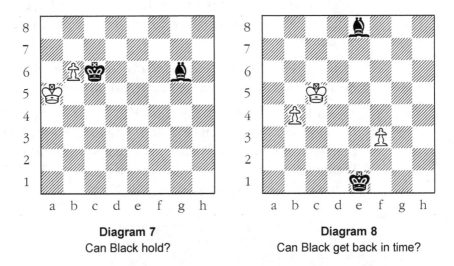

Diagram 7
Can Black hold?

Diagram 8
Can Black get back in time?

A bishop has problems stopping two passed pawns when his king is outside the square of both. From Diagram 8 Black scrapes back in time.

1...Ke2 2 f4 Ke3 3 f5 Ke4 4 f6 Ke5 5 b5 Now if Black captures on f6 then 6 b6 queens, or if he captures on b5 then 6 f7 will win, but he can draw by **5...Ke6! 6 b6 Kd7 7 Kb5 Kc8+ 8 Ka6 Kb8** and draws. An instructive king walk!

We have already seen that bishop and 'wrong rook's pawn' doesn't win if the opposing king gets to the corner. However there is another, rarer, draw with the same material.

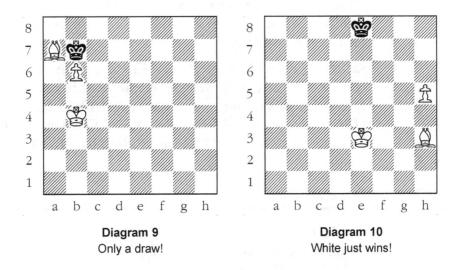

Diagram 9
Only a draw!

Diagram 10
White just wins!

White cannot undertake anything positive in Diagram 9 because of stalemate, as Black can defend by shuffling between a8 and b7.

In Diagram 10, as we have already seen, Black draws *if he gets his king to the corner*. Here White can prevent it.

1 Be6 Ke7 Or 1...Kf8 2 h6. **2 h6 Kf6 3 Bf5** Stopping the king from getting to g6. **3...Kf7 4 Bh7!** Creating a barrier on the g-file. **4...Kf6 5 Kf4** and White arrives just in time to close out the black king. The game could continue 5...Kf7 6 Kf5 Kf8 7 Kf6 Ke8 8 Kg7 Ke7 9 Bf5 etc.

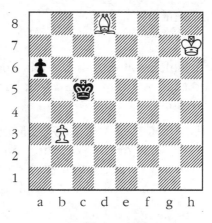

Diagram 11
Holding up the queenside

Black is a piece down but hopes to draw by eliminating the last white pawn or converting it into an a-pawn so that he can head to the corner and draw.

1 Ba5! 1 Be7+? Kb5 2 Kg6 a5 3 Kf5 a4 only draws. **1...Kb5 2 b4!** and White calmly brings his king over to take the a-pawn. Black can do nothing, a plausible finish being 2...Kc6 3 Kg6 Kb5 4 Kf5 Kc6 5 Ke6 Kb7 6 Kd7 Ka7 7 Kc6 Kb8 8 Kb6 Ka8 9 Kxa6 Kb8 10 b5 Ka8 11 b6 Kb8 12 Bd2 Ka8 13 b7+ Kb8 14 Bf4 mate.

Rooks and Pawns

In the ending of rook against pawn, the question is normally whether or not the rook and king can stop the pawn in time and win. If not, then it's a draw.

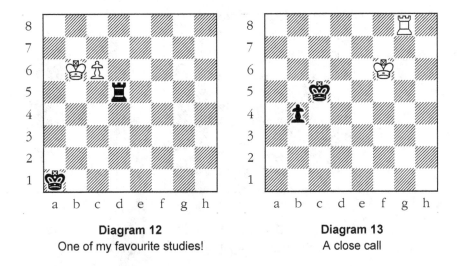

Diagram 12
One of my favourite studies!

Diagram 13
A close call

In Diagram 12 (a study by Saavendra) we see a rare win for the pawn, which illustrates an important point:

A rook is a long-range piece and does not feel comfortable near the opposing king.

1 c7 Rd6+ Otherwise White queens. **2 Kb5!** With 2 Kb7 Rd7 and 2 Kc5 Rd1 Black saves the game. **2...Rd5+ 3 Kb4! Rd4+ 4 Kb3! Rd3+ 5 Kc2** Only now when Black cannot threaten a skewer on the c-file does White come to the c-file. **5...Rd4!** So that if 6 c8Q then 6...Rc4+ is stalemate! **6 c8R!** Stopping ideas of stalemate and threatening mate on the a-file. **6...Ra4 7 Kb3** With two threats: mate and the rook. White wins. The king really dominated Black's rook!

TIP: Ideally rooks are best-placed well out of arm's reach of the opposing king.

In Diagram 13 the white king should come back as quickly as possible. The rook will come to the b-file in good time, but it is best to do so with gain of time. Black should advance his pawn with his king in close support.

1 Ke5 It's instructive that 1 Rb8 is too slow: 1...Kc4 2 Ke5 b3 3 Ke4 Kc3 4 Ke3 b2 5 Ke2 Kc2 6 Rc8+ Kb3 and White can no longer win. **1...Kc4 2 Ke4 Kc3 3 Ke3 b3 4 Rc8+** Now Black loses time by blocking his own pawn. **4...Kb2 5 Kd2 Ka2 6 Rb8 Kb2 7 Rb7 Ka2 8 Kc3** and wins.

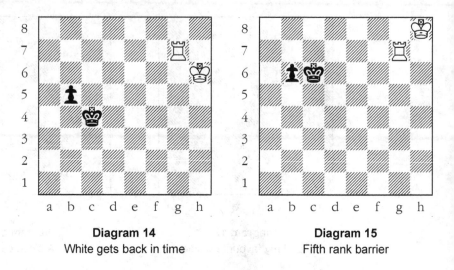

Diagram 14
White gets back in time

Diagram 15
Fifth rank barrier

In Diagram 14 White to play can just about win. As Black's king is ideally placed, the rook approaches with an annoying check.

1 Rc7+ Kd3 Or 1...Kb3 when White's king can race back: 2 Kg5 b4 3 Kf4 Ka2 4 Ke3 b3 5 Ra7+ Kb1 6 Kd2 b2 7 Rb7 Ka2 8 Kc2 **2 Rb7 Kc4 3 Kg5 b4 4 Kf4 Kc3 5 Ke3 b3 6 Rc7+** White then wins as in the previous example.

In Diagram 15 White's king is very far away, but he still wins. **1...b5** Or 1...Kc5 2 Rc7+ as in the previous example. The rook gains time to get behind the pawn. **2 Rg5!** The barrier on the fifth rank is an effective method. **2...Kb6** Slow but after 2...b4 3 Kg7 b3 4 Rg3! b2 5 Rb3 White simply wins the pawn. **3 Kg7 Ka5 4 Kf6 Kb4** Trying to hold up the white king's approach. Instead after 4...Ka4 5 Ke5 b4 6 Kd4 b3 7 Kc3 White wins more quickly. **5 Ke5 Kc3 6 Rg3+ Kc4 7 Ke4 b4 8 Ke3 Kc3 9 Rg8** with a familiar win (if you have studied the previous two examples!).

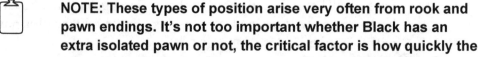

NOTE: These types of position arise very often from rook and pawn endings. It's not too important whether Black has an extra isolated pawn or not, the critical factor is how quickly the pawn (or in the case of two or more; the most dangerous pawn) can advance compared with the retreat of the white king.

See the ending Van Mil-Flear (from Chapter Eight) for an example where Black was successful in holding the draw.

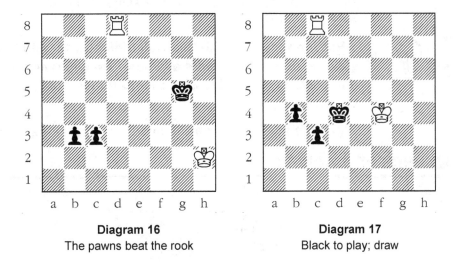

Diagram 16
The pawns beat the rook

Diagram 17
Black to play; draw

A rook cannot handle two connected passed pawns on the sixth (Diagram 16).

1 Rc8 c2 2 Kg2 b2 3 Rxc2 b1Q and Black has a theoretical win, as we saw in Chapter Two.

With pawns on the fifth rank White has no problems holding a draw if his king is fairly close.

In Diagram 17 the importance of the position of White's king should not be underestimated. Pick up the white king and read on!

If the white king were placed instead on, say, b3 then he just blocks the pawns and wins. If he were far away on h6 then the black army would be too strong for the rook and Black would win.

Returning to Diagram 17 (with the king back on f4!) the result is decided by who is to move. With White to play he has time to win.

1 Rd8+ Kc4 2 Ke3 Kb3 Or 2...b3 3 Rc8+ Kb4 4 Kd3. **3 Rb8 Kc4 4 Ke2 b3 5 Kd1 b2 6 Kc2 Kd4 7 Rb3** with zugzwang, White captures the c-pawn next move.

From the diagram with Black to move then... **1...Kd3** ...typically will lead to... **2 Rd8+ Kc2 3 Rb8 b3 4 Ke3 b2 5 Kd4 b1Q 6 Rxb1 Kxb1 7 Kxc3** and draws.

TIP: In judging rook against pawn(s) the main question to ask oneself is 'Can White's king get back in time?'

Don't forget to take into account some of the ideas examined here to gain time.

TIP: When playing with the rook look how to gain time by slowing down the pawn's advance. Take into account barriers and disruptive checks. Pick the right moment to come behind the pawn.

If playing with the pawn the handling of the king is important.

Queens and Pawns

Diagram 18
The queen beats a knight's pawn

With a knight's pawn (b- or g-pawn) the win is slow but sure. White forces his opponent's king in front of the pawn and then brings up his own king to prepare a mating net.

1 Qc7+ Kd2 2 Qb6 Kc2 3 Qc5+ Kb3 4 Qb5+ Kc2 5 Qc4+ Kd2 6 Qb3 Kc1 7 Qc3+ Kb1 Now the king comes nearer. **8 Kg7 Ka2 9 Qc2 Ka1 10 Qa4+ Kb1 11 Kf6 Kc1 12 Qc4+ Kd2 13 Qb3 Kc1 14 Qc3+ Kb1 15 Ke5 Ka2 16 Qc2 Ka1 17 Qa4+ Kb1 18 Kd4 Kc1 19 Kc3!** The quickest. Alternatively 19 Qc4+ Kd2 20 Qb3 Kc1 21 Qc3+ Kb1 22 Kc4 Ka2 23 Qa5+ Kb1 24 Kb3 Kc1 25 Qe1 mate. **19...b1Q 20 Qf4+ Kd1 21 Qd2 mate**.

It doesn't matter where the white king finds itself, the queen can always gain time to enable the king to saunter closer until the mating net is good and ready. With a bishop's pawn (c- or f-pawn) there is however a saving resource (Diagram 19).

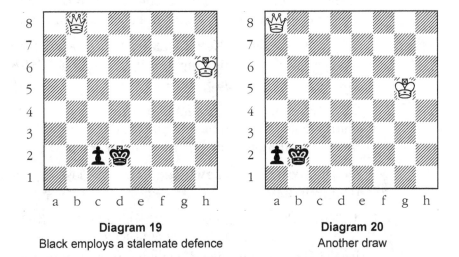

Diagram 19
Black employs a stalemate defence

Diagram 20
Another draw

1 Qb2 Kd1 2 Qd4+ Ke2 3 Qc3 Kd1 4 Qd3+ Kc1 So far as in the previous example, but here there is a catch! **5 Kg5 Kb2 6 Qd2 Kb1 7 Qb4+ Ka1 8 Qc3+ Kb1 9 Qb3+ Ka1!** That's it! White can't take the pawn in view of stalemate and cannot gain any further time, so it's a draw!

The rook's pawn also gives stalemate chances (Diagram 20). **1 Qb7+ Ka1** and again White cannot make progress.

NOTE: With queen against a pawn on the seventh rank; on files b-, d-, e- and g- White wins; on files a-, c-, f-, h- it is a draw unless the white king is very close by. When anticipating pawn races, take this rule into account.

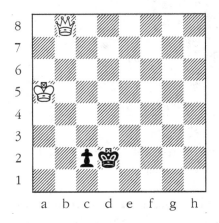

Diagram 21
Close enough to mate!

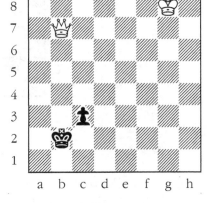

Diagram 22
Pawn on the sixth

If the white king were any further away in Diagram 21 then the game would be drawn. Here he can organise a win:

1 Qb2 Kd1 2 Qd4+ Ke2 3 Qc3 Kd1 4 Qd3+ Kc1 White's only chance to bring up his king, but it's enough. **5 Kb4 Kb2 6 Qd2 Kb1 7 Kb3 c1Q 8 Qa2 mate**.

These endings are very common. Typically a race in a pawn ending has been won by one player, but only just, and he then has to try and beat the advanced opposing pawn.

On the sixth rank, a pawn *almost always* loses against a queen (Diagram 22).

1...Kc1 Others are no better: 1...Ka3 2 Qb1; 1...Kc2 allows 2 Kf7; and 1...Ka1 2 Qg7 Kb2 3 Qd4 Kb3 4 Kf7 c2 5 Qa1 is hopeless. **2 Qh1+** Otherwise Black advances his pawn with a draw. **2...Kb2** After 2...Kd2 White approaches with checks before pinning on the diagonal: 3 Qg2+ Kc1 4 Qf1+ Kd2 5 Qf2+ Kc1 6 Qe3+ Kb2 7 Qd4. **3 Qh8!** A long diagonal indeed! In fact the pin is deadly. **3...Kb3 4 Kf7 c2 5 Qa1** and it's all over.

NOTE: Pinning the pawn on the diagonal is a useful tactic.

The only exception I know to the rule 'A pawn on the sixth always loses' is the following position.

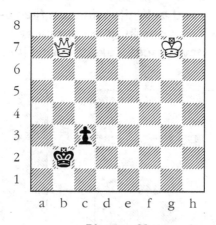

Diagram 23
A remarkable exception.

Compared to the previous position we can see that White's king is closer, but the diagonal pin is impossible and Black just about holds on.

1...Kc1 2 Qh1+ Kb2 3 Qb7+ Kc1 and the threat of ...c3-c2 is enough to hold.

This example induces me to make a new rule 'In chess there are exceptions to all rules!'. So

WARNING: Blindly following rules from books is not the way to improve.

Understanding why manoeuvres, zugzwangs, resources, and plans work in a given example will help you to apply them to appropriate circumstances in your own games.

Try it Yourself

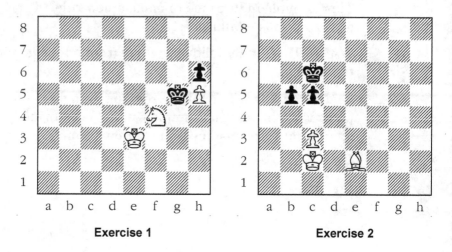

Exercise 1

Exercise 2

Exercise 1: Can White to play win?

Exercise 2: Can Black to play draw?

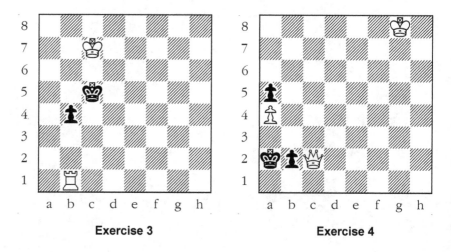

Exercise 3

Exercise 4

Exercise 3: What result with a) White to play? b) Black to play?

Exercise 4: What result with a) White to play? b) Black to play?

Summary

With few pawns remaining be aware of possible special drawing resources.

An advanced or distant passed pawn can sometimes hold even
against a rook or queen.

A minor piece and pawn doesn't always beat a bare king.

Chapter Eleven

Practical Advice

- **How should I study?**
- **Practical Tips**
- **Try it Yourself**

In any physical or mental activity some preparation or training is necessary, so perhaps the question should be 'How should I study to enable me to improve my play?' If you prefer to play rather than open chess books, but have made an exception for me (thanks anyway!), you would like me really to answer 'What practical steps should I take during games to get the best out of my endgame positions?'

To satisfy both types of enthusiast I shall try and answer both.

How should I study the Endgame?

1. Your own games are full of lessons for the future!

Indulge in a post-mortem with your opponent after the game, as he may have viewed the ending differently from you. Later, review and test any analysis you made during the game or with your opponent in the post-mortem, focusing on the critical moments in the ending. Try and remember if your thoughts during the game were more or less on the right lines or misdirected.

You can try and find a similar position to compare it with, perhaps from an endgame book, on a chess computer database or even in a master game you remember.

Make some conclusions and show your analysis to a friend who may try and refute or at least improve on your ideas. If the opponent in the game is available tell him that you could have won with such-and-such a move because of such-and-such a reason. Two days later he may come back to you with a defensive idea. It's almost like conducting a scientific piece of analysis!

This is how masters seek the truth in a key position whether it is in the opening or the ending. They then go one stage further; they publish their work, opening themselves up to further comments and criticism. Having to avoid making a fool of yourself in print is a sure way of motivating a conscientious player to verify that the analysis is of good quality!

2. Don't forget the great masters

I recommend that you study master games – and not just for

the opening! If you come to an interesting ending, cover the page and take the time to study it alone, reach your own conclusions, write them down and compare your ideas with those of the game continuation.

You may see a line of analysis or just a comment which looks unconvincing. Don't stop there, take a deeper look! Try and find an improvement or a refutation of their work.

Take note of their comments on aspects of play such as which pieces to exchange and why, the choice of plan, restricting the opponent's counterplay, improving piece placements etc.

3. Try to solve endgame exercises

There are forty in this book of varying degrees of difficulty. That should get you started, but you will find others in magazines, newspapers and other books etc.

Set some endgame exercises for a friend, he will do the same for you. Solving practical-looking positions is great fun, but really helps you learn. Nobody said that studying has to be dull!

4. Work on your weaknesses!

If your play, or work on analysing games, shows up a lack of understanding in a particular type of ending, let's say you just seem to get queen endings wrong, do something about it!

Firstly recognise your weakness, then get some practical examples from a book or a computer and concentrate your study on them.

If an athlete has a weak muscle he will do extra body-building on that weak point. Chessplayers should do the same.

5. Quality not quantity

Imagine that you spend a weekend playing quickly through 100 theoretical positions from a large endgame reference book and a friend spends the same amount of time analysing in detail all the ramifications of just 10. Three months later who would have remembered, and more importantly, learnt the most? In my experience quality helps one learn better than quantity, understanding what is going on rather than just memorising, will better prepare you for applying your studies to competitive games.

6. Read this book!

Practical Tips for the Heat of Battle

1. Cool down!

When you first enter the ending, after the exchange of some pieces, the character of the position has changed. If you have time, take a breather and then come back to the board afresh and try and judge the ending objectively. After the time control, again if you have time, take another 'time-out'.

2. Make a rough sketch

An artist will pencil in a rough image before later concentrating on the fine detail of colour and light. In the same way, look first at what *general aims and options* you and your opponent have in the position. See if you should first try and *stop your opponent* before pressing on with your own ideas. If you are not sure who is better, first of all try to see if you have a variation or manoeuvre that equalises, if so, try and see if you can play for more.

3. Use all of your pieces

Look how you can *improve the worst placed of your pieces*, not forgetting the king. Once you have an idea of what your assets are realistically capable of then *formulate a plan* of action with a longer-term aim as well as a series of mini-plans to solve short-term problems.

4. Active or passive?

You may now or at some future point have to make a stark decision between a defensive, passive plan and burning bridges to activate your pieces. Try to be ready and to view the circumstances when it will be the right moment to hit the active button, e.g. you may conclude 'I'm itching to sac my weak pawn to go active but it'll more effective when his king is further away, so I'll wait until his king gets to the d6-square.'

5. Organise your thinking

If you find it hard to separate planning from analysing variations then *split your thinking time into two*: when it is your
turn to move, concentrate on variations, when it is your opponent's turn to move, concentrate on general considerations and
a review of your plans.

6. Slow but sure

When manoeuvring if your opponent can undertake nothing
positive and is just waiting then *take your time*. If you have a
comfortable but rather slow win, that's good enough, don't be
tempted by a flashy but risky attempt to speed up the process.

7. Don't lose the thread

When analysing forcing variations, don't lose sight of your plan
by simply playing for cheap tactical tricks. *Keep your aims in
mind* and look for a sensible way of carrying them out. *Don't be
distracted* from a good plan by fantasy variations.

8. Use your book knowledge

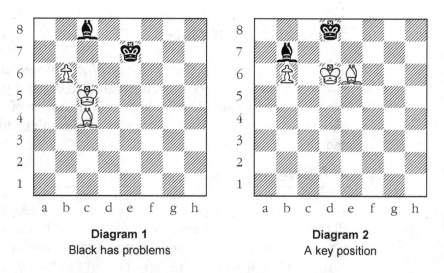

Diagram 1
Black has problems

Diagram 2
A key position

Compare the present position and others, arising from plausible simplification, with what you already know about endings. This may help you decide which pieces you should exchange and which to keep. Diagram 1 shows an example from my playing career of how I applied some of these points to solving practical problems. Going into the last round of a tournament, I was rather surprisingly leading, half a point ahead of two or three players including my opponent. I hadn't played particularly well in this important game (Vukic-Flear, Hem 1984) and from Diagram 1 I folded badly.

1...Bb7? 2 Bd5! Ba6 Unfortunately after 2...Bxd5 3 Kxd5 Kd7 White obtains the opposition and wins with 4 Kc5! Kd8 5 Kd6 Kc8 6 Kc6 Kb8 7 b7. **3 Kc6 Kd8 4 Be6 Bd3 5 Kb7** and I resigned in view of 5...Be4+ 6 Ka7 Bf3 7 Bc4 Kc8 8 Ba6+ Kd8 9 Bb7 Bg4 10 Bd5 Bc8 11 Be6.

I was unhappy with a probable draw that I had missed earlier and with my performance at the end. In particular I was kicking myself for not having played 1...Kd7, as I wasn't sure if this led to a draw or not.

I spent some time on this ending and over the next week or so I showed some of my lines to friends, who occasionally found refinements. When I returned home I looked in Averbakh's *Bishop Endings* and found a similar position which confirmed most of my own discoveries. A concise analysis of this ending runs as follows: 2 Bb5+ Kd8 3 Kc6! Bd7+ (on 3...Bh3 4 Kb7 and wins as in the game) 4 Kd6 Bc8 (4...Bh3 fails to the remarkable 5 b7! Bc8 6 b8B!! No, this isn't a misprint, White must underpromote to a bishop to win.) 5 Bd7 Ba6 (on 5...Bxd7 then 6 b7 or 5...Bb7 6 Be6! with zugzwang, see Diagram 2) 6 Bf5 Bb7 (6...Bb5 7 b7 or 6...Bc8 7 Bxc8 Kxc8 8 Kc6) 7 Be6!

Once I understood that this position is zugzwang then many things became clear. Black to play loses, White to play cannot win. Basically if White plays Bd5 at any point then Black must have his bishop *already on b7* and react with ...Kc8. White's bishop must stop ...Kc8 at virtually all times, so to threaten Bd5, and also defend the c8 square, the bishop must be on e6. So if White puts his bishop on e6 Black must *then and only then* react with ...Bb7. In Vukic-Flear, White can obtain this position with Black to play. Play continues from Diagram 2 with 7...Ba6 (7...Bf3 8 Bd5!) 8 Kc6 Be2 9 Kb7! as in the game. So I concluded that 1...Kd7 was more robust but still lost.

This was not the end of the story. A year or so later I was struggling against another Yugoslav in Paunovic-Flear, Geneva 1986.

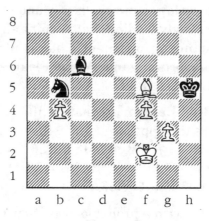

Diagram 3
Black is struggling

I'm not sure whether Black is lost or not here. However, it felt very uncomfortable at the time! Just look at what happened in the game. I was able to apply the knowledge that I had learnt from the analysis of the Vukic ending to great effect.

1 Ke3 Nd6 2 g4+ Kh6 3 Bd3 Bd7 4 g5+ Kh5 5 Kd4 Kg4 6 Ke5 Nf7+ 7 Kf6 Kxf4 8 Kxf7 Kxg5 9 Ke7 Ba4 10 Kd6 Kf6 11 Bc4 Be8 12 Bd5 Bb5 13 Kc5 Be2 14 Bc4 Bd1 15 b5 Ke7 16 b6 Kd8 17 Be6 Bf3 18 Kd6 Bb7 A familiar position! This time my opponent was in zugzwang! **19 Bf5 Bf3 20 Bd7 Be4 21 Bg4 Bg2 22 Be6** Now there is only one square. **22...Bb7!** Of course, repeating the zugzwang! **23 Kc5 Bf3 24 Bd5 Bg4 25 Bb7 Be2 26 Kb4 Bf1 27 Ka5 ½-½**

A satisfying half-point. From the above diagram I knew which position I was heading for and I got there! I would never have learnt this type of ending so well if I hadn't followed my own advice from some of the tips given above. So my final tip is:

TIP: Read the tips and follow them, they really do help you improve your endings!

Chapter Twelve

Solutions to Exercises

Chapter One: Solutions

Exercise 1

White is a pawn down, but has a great opportunity to turn the tables with **1 b5!** when he obtains an unstoppable passed pawn.

Exercise 2

If White simplifies to a rook ending or alternatively avoids the exchange of bishops with 1 Bc4 the position is about equal. However, he has the possibility to simplify to a pawn ending where his king is the most active. Analysis shows that this wins after **1 Rxf7! Rfxf7 2 Rf1 Kf8 3 Bxf7 Rxf7 4 Rxf7+ Kxf7 5 Kc3 Ke6** Black is far too slow in the race after 5...Kf6 6 Kc4 Kg5 7 Kb5 Kxh5 8 Kxb6 Kg4 9 a5 h5 10 a6 Kxg3 11 a7 h4 12 a8Q. **6 Kc4 Kd6 7 Kb5 Kc7 8 a5!** Leading to the win of a pawn. **8...bxa5 9 Kxc5 Kb7 10 Kb5 Ka7 11 Kxa5** winning easily.

TIP: Look out for combinations that simplify advantageously.

Exercise 3

This is a position from analysis of Keres-Fischer, Curaçao 1962. White can force a draw as follows: **1 Bf5+ Kh6** After 1...Qxf5+ 2 Qxf5+ Qg6 3 Qxg6+ Kxg6 White takes the 'opposition' and draws with 4 Kg4. See Chapter Three for further examples of this theme. **2 Qf6+ Kh5 3 Bg6+! Qxg6 4 Qg5+!** forcing stalemate!

Exercise 4

Black found a nice win in Cebalo-Flear, Asti 1998.

34...Bf4! 35 Rxf4 35 h5 offers more resistance, but after 35...Bxg3 36 Rxg4 Bc7+ 37 Kh4 Bd8+ 38 Rg5 Rxb3 39 Rxe6 Rb4+ 40 Kg3 Bxg5 Black wins comfortably. **35...Rc1 36 Rxg4 Rh1 mate**.

TIP: Don't forget that many endings require a tactical solution and that mate is the ultimate tactic!

Chapter Two: Solutions

Exercise 1

1 Kb6 Bringing up the king and limiting Black to two squares. **1...Kc8 2 Bb5 Kb8 3 Ba6** Black has only b8 and a8 in which to manoeuvre whilst White reorganises his pieces for the knock-out blow. **3...Ka8 4 Nd4 Kb8 5 Nc6+ Ka8 6 Bb7 mate**. So White mates in *six* moves.

Exercise 2

After **1 Bf4!** White threatens mate and there is no way to resist: **1...Kf8 2 Bd6+ Ke8 3 Rg8+ Rf8 4 Rxf8 mate**.

Exercise 3

Following **1...Bb8** White has **2 Qb4+ Ka8 3 Kc8** and with the king so close Black is in a mating net. **3...Ba7 4 Kc7 Bh1 5 Qf8+ Bb8+ 6 Qxb8 mate**.

Exercise 4

It is simplest to pass the move back to Black: **1 Qe8+ Kc7 2 Qe5+ Kc8 3 Qe7** and wins as in the variations given in the question.

Chapter Three: Solutions

Exercise 1

White goes around the g-pawn: **1 Kf2 Kd6 2 Kg3 Ke5 3 Kh4 Kf6 4 Kh5 Kg7** and wins by taking the opposition with... **5 Kg5**.

Exercise 2

Yes, as the pawns do not mutually protect each other for long: **1...Ka5 2 d5 Kb6!** 2...Kxa4? fails to 3 d6. **3 Kb2 Kc5 4 Kc3 Kxd5 5 Kb4 Kc6** with an easy draw as the remaining pawn is an a-pawn.

Exercise 3

It's enough. **1 Kf6 Kf4 2 Ke6 Ke4 3 Kd6 Kd4 4 Kc6 Kc3 5 Kxb6 Kxb3** and now zugzwang with... **6 Kb5!** ...decides the game. **6...Kc3** Or 6...Ka3 7 Kxa5. **7 Kxc5 etc.**

Exercise 4

Yes, by **1 c7+ Kc8 2 Kd5!** 2 Kc6? is stalemate. **2...Kxc7** 2...Kd7 3 c8Q+ Kxc8 4 Kc6 changes very little. **3 Ke6** Black is outmanoeuvred: **3...Kb7 4 Kd7 Kb8 5 Kc6 Ka7 6 Kc7 Ka8 7 Kxb6 Kb8 8 Ka6 Ka8 9 b6 Kb8 10 b7** and wins.

Chapter Four: Solutions

Exercise 1

There is the immediate **1 Nxb7! Nxb7 2 a6** and the pawn queens. A useful little combination to remember!

Exercise 2

1...Kb4 ...should be met by... **2 Kb6 Kc4 3 Nc3!** This forces the knight to release its grasp on the a7-square. The knight is then eased away by the king after **3...Nd6 4 Kc7! Ne8+ 5 Kc6 Kxc3 6 a7** and White queens.

Exercise 3

White should not play the obvious 1 b5? as after 1...Nxb5 2 Kxb5 the black king cannot be forced out of the corner as, if White approaches the h-pawn, then stalemate occurs. Instead... **1 Ne4!** ...is the way to win. White's plan is to chase the opposing knight away from the b-pawn. **1...Kxh7 2 Nd2 Kg7 3 Nc4 Nb1** After 3...Nc2 4 b5 Ne1 5 b6 Nd3+ 6 Kb5 the pawn will run to b8. **4 Kd4!** Rather limiting the black knight! **4...Kf7 5 b5 Ke7 6 b6 Kd7 7 Kc5 Nc3 8 Ne5+ Kc8 9 Kc6** and the threat of b7+ followed by Nd7+ is decisive.

Exercise 4

White wins with... **1 Ka2!** ...putting Black in zugzwang **1...Kh4** 1...Ne5 2 Ne7 and 1...Kf4 2 Nf6 Ne7 3 Nd5+! Nxd5 4 g8Q are no better. **2 Nh6 Ne7 3 Nf5+! Nxf5 4 g8Q** with an easy win.

Chapter Five: Solutions

Exercise 1

Yes, but only by precise play. **1 Bd2** Must be met by... **1...Kf8!** Otherwise White has 2 Bh6 and 3 Bg7 followed by the decisive advance of the f-pawn. **2 Bg5 Kg8!** A light square! Not 2...Bc3 3 Bf6 Be1 4 Bg7+ Ke8 5 f6 and White will eventually win. **3 Bf6 Bf2 4 Be5 Bh4 5 Bf4 Be7 6 Bg5 Bxg5! 7 Kxg5 Kf7** and draws. The proximity of the king enabled simplification into a drawn pawn ending.

Exercise 2

Yes, and the technique involved is instructive. **1...Ke4 2 Kg2 Kd3 3 Kf1 Bc3 4 Bd8 Bb4 5 Bf6 Kc2** Black heads for a set-up of the king on b3 and the bishop on b2. **6 Ke2 Kb3** If White could now play his king to c1 he would draw as in the solution to the previous exercise. **7 Be5 Ba3 8 Bf6 Bb2 9 Bg5 c3 10 Bh6 c2 11 Kd3 Ba3 12 Bg5 Kb2 13 Kc4 Kb1 14 Kb3 Bc1 15 Be7 Bh6 16 Ba3 Bf8 17 Bb2 Be7** And White has no moves. The a3-c1 diagonal is too short.

Exercise 3

A typical 'good' vs. 'bad' bishop position. Karpov soon had Hort in zugzwang (Budapest 1973). **1 Ke3 Bg4 2 Bd3 Be6 3 Kd4 Bg4 4 Bc2** Threatening 5 Bb3. **4...Be6 5 Bb3 Bf7 6 Bd1** Heading for g4. **6...Be6 7 Bf3** Zugzwang; if the king moves, White's monarch invades. **7...Bf7 8 Bg4** Black resigned. After 8...Be6 9 Bxe6 Kxe6 10 g4 Kd6 11 a3 the pawn ending is won. Otherwise 8...Bg8 9 Bc8 Bf7 10 Bxa6 is pretty grim, e.g. 10...Be8 11 Bc8 Bf7 12 f5 Be8 13 f6 Bf7 14 Bg4 Be8 15 Be2 Bc6 16 f7 Ke7 17 Kc5 with a comfortable win.

Exercise 4

White can draw! **1 Bd1 Kc3 2 Bc2!** and the bishop cannot be captured in view of stalemate. But not 2 Bg4? Kb2 3 Bd1 Kxa3 winning for Black. **2...Kb2** Or 2...Be8 3 Bd1 Bd7 4 Bf3 Bb5 5 Bd1 and Black isn't getting anywhere. **3 Bxa4! Bxa4 4 Ke2**

Eliminating the last pawn.

Chapter Six: Solutions

Exercise 1

A draw. 1 Kc5 Ke6 etc., and the white king is denied entry into the black camp.

Exercise 2

A win as Black has no problem advancing up the board in support of his pawns. Note that he has the 'right' rook's pawn and that four files separate the pawns, this is too wide a front for the defence. The game Forintos-Taimanov, Skopje 1970, continued **1...Ke6 2 Bf8 Kd5 3 Kg2 c5 4 Kf2 h5 5 Be7 Bd3 6 Ke3 c4 7 Bh4 Ke5 8 Be1 Kf5 9 Kf3 Be4+** The white king must commit itself. **10 Ke3** After 10 Kg3 Bd5 11 Kh4 Bf3 12 Kg3 Ke4 13 Bb4 Bg4 14 Ba5 Kd3 the c-pawn advances. **10...Bd5 11 Bg3 Kg4 12 Bd6 h4 13 Be5 Bf7 14 Bc3 Bg6 15 Be5 Be8** There is no hurry. **16 Bc3 Bb5 17 Bd2 h3 18 Kf2 Bc6** and White resigned as 19 Kg1 Kf3 20 Kh2 Bd7 21 Kg1 Ke2 22 Ba5 Kd3 23 Be1 c3 24 Bxc3 Kxc3 is an easy win.

Exercise 3

Black has a surprising win based on zugzwang. **1...g1Q! 2 Bxg1 Kg2** For White to draw, the bishop must stay on g1 and the white king must maintain an attack on the h3-pawn. However, Black just runs his opponent out of moves. **3 Kg4 Bc6 4 Kh4 Bf3! 5 a8Q Bxa8 6 Kg4 Bb7 7 Kh4 Bf3** Zugzwang. If the king moves then 8...Kxg1 wins.

Exercise 4

Averbakh showed how to create the second passed pawn which does in fact win the game. **1 g4! hxg4 2 h5 gxh5 3 a8Q Bxa8 4 Kxf5** Black's pawns are stymied. White eventually wins despite some technical problems: **4...Kf7 5 Kg5 Bf3 6 a7 Ba8 7 Bh4 Bf3 8 f5 Kg7 9 Bg3 Kf7 10 Be5 Be4 11 Kxh5** Only now, when everything is under control, has the moment come to take the pawn. **11...g3 12 Bxg3! Kf6 13 Kg4 Bxf5+ 14 Kf4** and queens the last pawn. If Black had taken the other way with 1...fxg4 then 2 f5 gxf5 3 Kxh5 Kf6 4 Bg3 Bf3 5 Kh6 Be4 6 h5 Bf3 7 Bh4+ Kf7 8 Kg5 Be4 9 Bg3 Kg7 10 Be5+ Kf7 11 h6 Kg8 12 a8Q+ Bxa8 13 Kg6 leads to a win for White.

Chapter Seven: Solutions

Exercise 1

White needs to get his king to c7 to control all of the knight's moves. **1 Kd5 Nb8 2 Ba7 Nd7 3 Kc6 Ne5+ 4 Kc7 Nd7 5 Bd4** and Black is fatally in zugzwang.

Exercise 2

Yes, by **1 Nb6!** Instead 1 Nc5 only draws after 1...Bc6 as further knight moves are met by ...Bxd7. **1...Bc6 2 Nd5+ Kd8 3 Kd6! Bxd7 4 e7+** Either king move is met by a fatal fork.

Exercise 3

It's drawn! The only try in Averbakh-Fridstein, Moscow 1947, is **1...g4** But then... **2 Kh4!** After 2 Ng2 Black has an instructive idea 2...e3! 3 Nxe3 Kg5 4 Ng2 Kf5 and the king invades. **2...Kg6 3 Kg3 Kh5 4 Ng2 Kg5 5 Ne3 Kg6 6 Kh4 Kf6 7 Kg3 Kg5 8 Ng2** and the blockade is maintained.

Exercise 4

This looks dangerous for Black, but he can draw by forcing a blockade. Remember that if White exchanges his g-pawn for the knight then a draw is inevitable as it's the 'wrong' rook's pawn. **1...Nh4+! 2 Kf2 Nf5** Threatening 3...Nxg3. **3 g4 Kf4! 4 Bd3 Nh4 5 Bc2 Nf3 6 Bd1 Nh4 7 Be2 Ng6 8 Bf1 Ne5 9 Be2 Ng6** and White cannot make progress.

Chapter Eight: Solutions

Exercise 1

In Botvinnik-Keres, The Hague 1948, Black's defence was too passive and after **1...Rd6 2 Rc5 Ra6 3 a4** White was able to win by strolling his king over to the a-pawn. Instead a more active approach was called for: **1...Rd4! 2 Rc6+ Kg7 3 Kh5 Rd3 4 a4 Rd4 5 Rc7+ Kf8! 6 g5 Rxa4 7 Kg6 Ra1** as now Black also has a passed pawn and draws easily.

TIP: When in doubt, activate the rook!

Exercise 2

White does have a passed d-pawn supported by his rook. However, it is isolated and Black's king can blockade it, in addition the b-pawns are weak whereas Black has a solid pawn structure.

Black is better and the game continuation of Torre-Miles, Amsterdam 1977, confirmed this: **1 d5** 1 Kf2 Kf8 2 Kf3 f5 doesn't help matters. **1...Kf8 2 d6 Ke8 3 Rc2** Trying to go active. **3...Rb4 4 Rc7 Rxb3 5 Re7+ Kf8 6 Rc7 Ke8 7 Re7+ Kd8! 8 Kf2** After 8 Rxf7 Rxb2 9 Rxh7 a5 the two connected passed pawns will win the day. **8...a5 9 Rxf7 a4 10 Rxh7 Rxb2+ 11 Kf3 a3 12 h4 Rb6!** Preparing to put the rook behind the pawn after 13 Rh8+ Kd7 14 Ra8 Ra6, so Torre resigned.

TIP: Look for weaknesses in the pawn structure.

Exercise 3

From the famous game Capablanca-Tartakower, New York 1924. White is better as he is able to use his king as an attacking force, combining well with his rook on the seventh and the passed g-pawn.

1 Kg3! Rxc3+ 2 Kh4 Rf3 3 g6 Rxf4+ 4 Kg5 Re4 Or 4...Rxd4 5 Kf6 Kg8 and 6 Rd7 mates! **5 Kf6!** Cunningly using the f-pawn as a shield. **5...Kg8 6 Rg7+ Kh8 7 Rxc7 Re8 8 Kxf5** It's time to cash in. **8...Re4 9 Kf6 Rf4+ 10 Ke5 Rg4 11 g7+ Kg8** The pawn ending would be hopeless. **12 Rxa7 Rg1 13 Kxd5 Rc1 14 Kd6 Rc2 15 d5 Rc1 16 Rc7 Ra1 17 Kc6 Rxa4 18 d6** and Black resigned.

A better defensive try was 2...a6!?, when the simplest for White is 3 Rd7! Rc4 (or 3...c6 4 g6 b5 5 axb5 axb5 6 Kg5 b4 7 Kf6 etc.) 4 Rxd5 Rxa4 5 Rxf5+ (5 g6 is less clear after 5...Ra5!?) 5...Kg7 6 Rd5 Rc4 7 f5 Rc1 8 Rd7+ Kg8 9 Kh5.

TIP: Activate the king!

Exercise 4

Degraeve-Flear, Montpellier 1996. White blundered with 1 Rc5? when 1...Rh6! 2 Kb5 Rb6+ won both pawns for a draw.

Pinter pointed out the win: **1 Rb6! Rh5+ 2 Kb4! Rh4+ 3 Kc3 Rh3+ 4 Kd2 Rh2+ 5 Ke1 Rh1+ 6 Kf2 Rh2+ 7 Kg3 Rh8 8 Rc6** and when the checks run out White will play Rc8 and the b-pawn will queen.

Chapter Nine: Solutions

Exercise 1

White has a centralised queen and a knight's pawn on the seventh rank. This is enough to win if his king can wriggle out of the checks. **1...Qf1+ 2 Qf4 Qb5+ 3 Kg4 Qe2+ 4 Qf3** Exploiting the theme of cross-checks; so 4...Qe6+ for instance is met by 5 Qf5+. **4...Qc4+ 5 Kg5 Qc1+ 6 Kf6 Qb2+** Black's available checks are less and less convincing! **7 Kf7 Qa2+ 8 Kf8** Stopping the checks and preparing for a new queen.

Exercise 2

Winning with a rook's pawn against a centralised queen can be difficult, if not impossible.

After **1...Qd2** White can give an annoying series of checks: **2 Qe5+ Kb1 3 Qb5+ Kc2 4 Qc4+ Kb2 5 Qb5+ Ka3 6 Qa6+ Kb3 7 Qe6+ Kb2 8 Qb6+ Kc2 9 Qc6+ Qc3 10 Qg6+ Kb2 11 Qb6+** Black's only shelter seems to be the a1-square which blocks his pawn. So, the game is drawn as Black cannot make progress.

Exercise 3

Yes, with **1...Qc7! 2 Ka6 Qc8+ 3 Ka5 Qc7** and Black uses the stalemate theme to draw.

In general, with two connected pawns on the a- and b-files (or g- and h-files) the win is usually comfortable if one takes care to avoid stalemate traps.

Exercise 4

White wins because of the strength of his passed pawn and Black's inability to create counterplay. **1 a6 Qa3** 1...Qa2 2 a7 e4 3 Qb7 e3 doesn't lead to perpetual check: 4 a8Q Qxf2+ 5 Kh3 Qf5+ 6 Kh2 Qf2+ 7 Qg2. **2 a7 e4 3 Qb8 Qf3+ 4 Kg1 Qd1+ 5 Kh2 Qe2 6 Qe5+ Kh7 7 Qf6** and Black can resign.

Chapter 10: Solutions

Exercise 1

The answer is no! The winning try... **1 Ke4 Kg4 2 Ke5 Kg5 3 Ke6 Kxf4 4 Kf6** ...fails to... **4...Ke4! 5 Kg6 Ke5 6 Kxh6 Kf6** White would win this way if the pawn were not a rook's pawn.

Exercise 2

Yes, he can! **1...Kb6 2 Kd3** After 2 Kb3 Ka5 3 Bf1 Kb6 4 Be2 Ka5 White cannot do anything as 5 Ka3 b4+ draws. **2...Ka5 3 Ke4 c4 4 Kd4 b4** This exchanges White's last pawn.

Exercise 3

Surprisingly enough, this is a zugzwang. Yes, with White to play it's only a draw and with Black to play White wins. Confused? Let's look at some lines. Firstly, with White to play: **1 Kb7 Kb5 2 Ka7** After 2 Rb2 Black gains time by later hitting the rook: 2...Kc4 3 Ka6 Kc3 4 Rh2 b3 5 Kb5 b2 and draws easily. **2...Ka5 3 Ra1+ Kb5** and White is getting nowhere. If in the original position it were Black to play: **1...Kb5 2 Kb7 Kc4 3 Ka6! b3 4 Ka5 Kc3 5 Ka4 b2 6 Ka3** and wins. Strange but true!

Exercise 4

White is denied use of the a4-square for a check and cannot win in the normal way against the b-pawn on the seventh. However, with White to play... **1 Kf7 Ka1 2 Ke6 b1Q 3 Qxb1+ Kxb1 4 Kd5 Kc2 5 Kc4** wins the pawn ending. With Black to play: White's king is too far away for the pawn ending and... **1...Ka1 2 Qc3 Ka2 3 Qxa5 b1Q** ...leads to a queen plus a-pawn against queen ending. Black has good drawing chances here as we saw in Chapter Nine.

CPSIA information can be obtained
at www.ICGtesting.com
Printed in the USA
BVHW061608210821
614260BV00004B/58